AF522678

HOW INDIA SCALED MT G20

PRAISE FOR THE BOOK

Amitabh Kant's firsthand account of India's G20 presidency provides a masterclass in leadership and diplomacy. With clarity and insight, this book captures India's pivotal role in navigating complex global challenges, driving inclusive growth and development, and fostering international cooperation. It offers a rare glimpse into the high-stakes decisions and visionary strategies that have not only raised India's stature still further but also reshaped the global narrative. A must-read for anyone seeking to understand how India is charting the course for a more resilient and interconnected world, and how the G20 can be led purposefully and effectively.

—**Nicholas Stern**, IG Patel Professor of Economics and Government; Chairman of the Grantham Research Institute on Climate Change and the Environment; and Head of the India Observatory at London School of Economics

The New Delhi G20 Leaders' Summit Declaration marks a defining moment in India's multilateral diplomacy, a remarkable achievement at a time when global consensus is increasingly elusive. Amitabh Kant, India's G20 Sherpa, provides an unparalleled inside story of how this bold vision for a more equitable world was realized. His deep expertise and nuanced understanding of global governance make this book both timely and essential. For anyone eager to grasp the intricacies of international diplomacy and India's leadership on the world stage, this is a must-read.

—**N. Chandrasekaran**, Chairman, Tata Sons

Nothing in recent times has helped reposition India on the global map more than its presidency of the G20. The contributions of this unusual Sherpa in forging consensus and handling complex negotiations, including on issues of multilateralism and building a resilient, cooperative world order, has no recent parallels. He was integral to India's success. This brilliantly written book captivates the dramas on and off stage. A compelling read.

—**N.K. Singh**, Co-Chair, G20 Independent Expert Group on MDB Reforms; President, Board of Trustees, Institute of Economic Growth; and Chairman, 15th Finance Commission, India

Amitabh Kant's book is a fascinating account of India's G20 presidency, where global governance and development converged under India's leadership. He brings forth an unparalleled understanding of complex negotiations and their far-reaching implications for the world economy. This book offers not just an insider's perspective, but also a broader vision of how India shaped new pathways for inclusive and sustainable growth.

—**Dr Arvind Panagariya**, Chairman, 16th Finance Commission of India; Jagdish Bhagwati Professor of Indian Political Economy at Columbia University; and India's G20 Sherpa from 2015 to 2017

In a world marked by geopolitical complexities and economic uncertainties, India's G20 presidency emerged as a beacon of hope and leadership. This book brilliantly captures how India navigated global challenges to advance a forward-looking agenda, focusing on growth, climate action and sustainable development. With its visionary leadership, India not only bolstered economic cooperation among nations, but also clinched the historic Green Development Pact, championing a path towards an inclusive, green economy. Amitabh Kant's insightful narrative provides a unique behind-the-scenes perspective on the negotiations and key decisions that will shape the global economic landscape for years to come. With its presidency of the G20, India has shown to the world that it is a rising superpower willing to cooperate to create bridges to resolve complex global challenges.

—**Nouriel Roubini**, Professor Emeritus, Stern School of Business, New York University

HOW INDIA SCALED MTG20

THE INSIDE STORY OF THE G20 PRESIDENCY

AMITABH KANT

RUPA

Published by
Rupa Publications India Pvt. Ltd 2025
7/16, Ansari Road, Daryaganj
New Delhi 110002

Sales centres:
Prayagraj Bengaluru Chennai
Hyderabad Jaipur Kathmandu
Kolkata Mumbai

Images courtesy: Author Archives/G20 India

P-ISBN: 978-93-6156-838-1
E-ISBN: 978-93-6156-513-7

Second impression 2025

10 9 8 7 6 5 4 3 2

Printed in India

CONTENTS

ABBREVIATIONS

ACs	Action councils
ADP	Aspirational Districts Programme
AI	Artificial intelligence
AMIS	Agricultural Market Information System
ASEAN	Association of Southeast Asian Nations
AU	African Union
BIS	Bank of International Settlements
BRI	Belt and Road Initiative
BSE	Bombay Stock Exchange
CADs	Current account details
CBDR	Common but differentiated responsibilities
CII	Confederation of Indian Industry
COP	Conference of the Parties
CSOD	Chair's Summary and Outcome Document
DBTs	Direct Benefit Transfers
DEPA	Data Empowerment and Protection Architecture
DIAL	Delhi International Airport Ltd
DMICDC	Delhi Mumbai Industrial Corridor Development Corporation
DMM	Development Ministers Meeting
DPI	Digital public infrastructure
DPIIT	Department of Industrial Policy and Promotion

DRR	Disaster risk reduction
DWG	Development Working Group
EAM	External Affairs Minister
EGs	Engagement Groups
ESG	Environment, Social and Governance
EVs	Electric vehicles
FAO	Food and Agriculture Organization
FSB	Financial Stability Board
FTE	Full-time equivalent
GBA	Global Biofuels Alliance
GDP	Gross domestic product
GDPIR	Global Digital Public Infrastructure Repository
GFC	Global Financial Crisis
GPFI	Global Partnership for Financial Inclusion
GPGs	Global public goods
GVCs	Global value chains
IAEA	International Atomic Energy Agency
IAF	Indian Air Force
IARI	Indian Agricultural Research Institute
IAS	Indian Administrative Service
IEA	International Energy Agency
IEG	Independent Expert Group
IFIs	International financial institutions
IFS	Indian Foreign Service
IGI	Indira Gandhi International Airport
ILO	International Labour Organization
IMEC	India-Middle East-Europe Economic Corridor
IMF	International Monetary Fund
IOs	International organizations
IoT	Internet of things
ISA	International Solar Alliance
IYM	International Year of Millets

KYC	Know your customer
LiFE	Lifestyle for Environment
LPG	Liquefied petroleum gas
LTCM	Long-Term Capital Management
MACS	Meeting of Agricultural Chief Scientists
MDBs	Multilateral development banks
MEA	Ministry of External Affairs
MeitY	Ministry of Electronics and Information Technology
MFO	Multinational Force and Observers
MICE	Meetings, incentives, conferences and exhibitions
ML	Machine learning
MOSIP	Modular Open-Source Identity Platform
MoUs	Memorandums of understanding
MP-IDSA	Manohar Parrikar Institute for Defence Studies and Analyses
MSMEs	Micro, small and medium enterprises
NDCs	Nationally determined contributions
NDLD	New Delhi Leaders' Declaration
NFHS	National Family Health Survey
NITI	National Institution for Transforming India
NRIs	Non-resident Indians
ODF	Open defecation-free
ODOP	One District One Product
OFA	One Future Alliance
ORF	Observer Research Foundation
PGII	Partnership for Global Infrastructure and Investment
PM	Prime Minister
PMJDY	Pradhan Mantri Jan-Dhan Yojana
PMMVY	Pradhan Mantri Matru Vandana Yojana
PMO	Prime Minister's Office

PMSMA	Pradhan Mantri Surakshit Matritva Abhiyan
PMUY	Pradhan Mantri Ujjwala Yojana
R&D	Research and development
SBM	Swachh Bharat Mission
SCO	Shanghai Cooperation Organisation
SDGs	Sustainable Development Goals
SIF	Social Impact Fund
T20	Think20
UK	United Kingdom
UNDP	United Nations Development Programme
UNEF	United Nations Emergency Force
UNFCCC	United Nations Framework Convention on Climate Change
UNGA	United Nations General Assembly
UNSC	United Nations Security Council
UPI	Unified Payments Interface
USA	United States of America
WGs	Working groups
WHO	World Health Organization

FOREWORD

DR S. JAISHANKAR
EXTERNAL AFFAIRS MINISTER OF INDIA

How India Scaled Mt G20 is a timely chronicle of India's leadership in turbulent times. In 2023, the year of India's presidency, the G20, as a major forum for global governance, faced significant challenges as our world navigated economic crises, major pandemics, climate calamities and geopolitical rifts. This book, authored by India's G20 Sherpa Amitabh Kant, tells the story of how India delivered success when it really mattered. In doing so, the importance of Prime Minister Narendra Modi's vision, decisiveness, and inclusive approach are highlighted.

India's presidency came at a pivotal moment. The world was still reeling from the prolonged aftershocks of the COVID-19 pandemic, with many countries facing rising inflation, supply chain disruptions, food and fertilizer crises and escalating inequalities. At the same time, climate change continues unabated, with extreme weather events becoming more frequent and devastating. Compounding these were significant geopolitical fractures, most notably the war in Ukraine, which added layers of complexity to already strained international relations. In such an environment, where multilateralism seemed to falter under the weight of competing interests and interlinked predicaments, India's G20 presidency stood out for its ability to harmonize interests and provide solutions for greater global good.

The core theme of India's presidency, rooted in the philosophy of '*Vasudhaiva Kutumbakam*—One Earth, One Family, One Future', was not just a slogan. It encapsulated India's aspirations to champion a new form of global cooperation—one that moved beyond the zero-sum politics that often define international relations. Under PM Modi's guidance, India positioned itself as a bridge, promoting healing in a world divided by geopolitical rifts, harmony amidst global discord, and hope for a sustainable and inclusive future.

How India Scaled Mt G20 takes us behind the scenes of India's presidency, highlighting how India worked tirelessly to promote inclusivity and dialogue. The Global South, long marginalized in global governance forums, found in India an advocate that understood its aspirations and challenges. During India's G20 presidency, we hosted the first-ever Voice of Global South Summit in January 2023. Through this process, we were able to highlight and discuss the central issues and priorities of the Global South. These insights then shaped our approach to the G20 discussions over the course of the year.

India's presidency was instrumental in elevating the African Union to full membership in the G20, a momentous step in reshaping global governance toward a more representative order, giving a voice to the 1.4 billion citizens of Africa. This act was more than symbolic; it underscored India's commitment to inclusivity, ensuring that the voices of the underrepresented were finally given the platform they deserved.

At the heart of India's G20 success was the visionary zeal of PM Modi. His unwavering focus on a human-centric approach to development and diplomacy proved crucial in building consensus on several contentious issues. One such triumph was India's leadership in advancing global climate action, culminating in the Green Development Pact. This was no easy task. At a time when nations were grappling with rising energy demands and the urgency to reduce carbon emissions, India, with its emphasis on sustainable development, navigated these challenges by striking a balance between economic growth and environmental stewardship.

The climate crisis, as outlined in this book, was a key focus of India's presidency. By promoting the Lifestyle for Environment (LiFE) initiative and pushing for ambitious targets, including tripling renewable energy capacity by 2030, India set the tone for a greener future. More importantly, India's efforts were not limited to rhetoric; they were backed by actionable solutions, such as promoting climate finance and supporting developing nations in their green transitions. Prime Minister Modi highlighted the importance of balancing competing priorities while never losing sight of long-term goals.

Kant also meticulously documents how India advanced the cause of digital transformation, particularly for the Global South. India's success in building digital public infrastructure (DPI) such as Aadhaar and UPI, which revolutionized financial inclusion, was presented as a model for other developing nations. Prime Minister Modi's belief in the power of technology as an equalizer was validated as India's DPI became a tool not just for economic growth, but also for ensuring that no one was left behind in the digital age. India's G20 presidency advanced this vision by promoting secure data governance and advocating for equitable access to digital technologies, laying the foundation for a digitally inclusive global economy.

India's G20 presidency was not without its challenges. The Russia-Ukraine conflict loomed large, threatening to derail global discussions on critical issues. Despite the complexities, India skilfully navigated the geopolitical tensions, maintaining a delicate balance between major global powers while steadfastly promoting the principles of peace and cooperation. Back-channel negotiations and alliances with emerging markets were crucial in keeping the dialogue open and productive.

As PM Modi has often remarked, leadership is not about avoiding challenges, but about confronting them head-on with courage and clarity of purpose. India's G20 presidency, as described in the concluding chapter of this book, exemplifies this spirit. Whether it was promoting gender equality and women-led development through the constitution of the Women's Empowerment Working Group or advancing the cause of the Global South, India's presidency demonstrated that true leadership lies in inclusivity—in ensuring that every voice, no matter how small, is heard.

In a rapidly changing world, where challenges continue to multiply, the lessons from India's G20 presidency will remain relevant for years to come. *How India Scaled Mt G20* is not just a record of past achievements but also a roadmap for the future. As India passes on the baton to future G20 presidencies, we do so with confidence that the principles of cooperation, inclusivity and sustainability that defined our leadership will continue to inspire global action.

I congratulate Amitabh Kant on this insightful account and commend his dedication towards ensuring the success of India's G20 journey. This work will serve as an invaluable resource for scholars, policymakers and leaders across the world, providing an insider's account of how India successfully scaled the Summit of the G20.

PROLOGUE

While the world was reeling under the challenges of a pandemic, climate change, economic uncertainty, trade and geopolitical tensions, India assumed the G20 presidency. As global leaders gathered to tackle crises from climate change to economic inequality, Prime Minister Narendra Modi sought not just to host the G20 but also to redefine its very purpose: from competition and self-interest to collaboration, inclusion and shared progress. Without the PM's leadership, the G20 would have drifted apart. During the G20 year, his instincts and judgements were critical, and he emerged as a primary strategist. In that capacity, PM Modi showed his great strength as a leader, inspiring all G20 leaders to walk alongside his vision of 'One Earth, One Family, One Future', or *Vasudhaiva Kutumbakam*, a Sanskrit phrase drawn from the *Maha Upanishad* which reflects the belief that the world is one interconnected family.

This phrase became the theme of our presidency. We embraced this philosophy as the cornerstone of our efforts, advocating unity amidst diversity and fostering collective responsibility to meet global challenges.

Throughout the presidency, India highlighted the urgent need to balance development with sustainability. These ideals align with the broader global agenda and offer an approach that seeks to reconcile growth with protecting the planet. Unprecedented initiatives marked the year of India's presidency, ranging from digital transformation to sustainable development and reform of multilateral institutions. As the book illustrates, India's presidency emphasized human-centric development, sustainability and inclusivity. India's vision extended beyond its borders by championing the voice of the Global South—those nations that often find themselves on the front lines of global crises yet historically excluded from key decision-making tables. India's presidency prioritized giving these countries a platform for articulating their needs and aspirations.

This book, *How India Scaled Mt G20*, chronicles the pivotal role India played in reshaping global governance and highlights the strategies that made its G20 presidency transformational. It details the behind-the-scenes efforts that crafted India's legacy at the G20, including the efforts of dedicated teams, diplomats and officers who, together, embodied the spirit of consensus and cooperation. It provides an insider's view of the intricate negotiations, the challenges faced, and the legacy left behind.

This is the story of how a nation, once seen as a developing power, rose to lead the world stage—offering solutions, forging alliances, and building a lasting legacy that reflects the aspirations of both developing and developed worlds.

ONE

NAVIGATING INTERNATIONAL WATERS

It was the summer of 2022. After seven long and fulfilling years as CEO of the National Institution for Transforming India (NITI) Aayog, my tenure came to an end in June. I thought my journey was heading towards a quiet denouement. But fate had other plans for me.

That month, I received an unexpected but fateful call from the Prime Minister's Office (PMO) asking me to attend a meeting with Prime Minister (PM) Narendra Modi. The atmosphere was bittersweet, not least because I was leaving behind a dedicated, young, and vibrant team and the legacy we had built together at NITI Aayog. Little did I know that this meeting would mark the beginning of a rapid transition in my career.

I was asked to step up to the role of a lifetime—take over as India's G20 Sherpa. The term 'Sherpa', though culturally anachronistic, was coined by policymakers to describe the personal representatives of leaders at the G20, drawing inspiration from the high-altitude guides of the Himalayas. It was my job to take India's leader to the top of a 'summit' of a different kind.

This role marked a significant transition and required me to switch gears quickly. My previous roles—from Sub-Collector in Thalassery and District Collector in Kozhikode in Kerala to starting vast infrastructural projects as Secretary of the Department of Industrial Policy and Promotion (DIPP, now DPIIT) and CEO of NITI Aayog, and driving grassroots implementation and transformative national policies—had always been deeply rooted within our borders. Now I was stepping onto a global stage where India's voice would resonate among the world's most influential economies. This was not just a unique professional opportunity, but also a historic moment for our country.

The Group of Twenty (G20) was a challenge of an entirely different magnitude—a complex global dance where each step required deft coordination and diplomatic finesse. Unlike the more familiar realm of local and national governance, steering the G20 meant plunging into a world where every move had to be calculated and every word carefully measured.

This required an intimate knowledge of treaties and past declarations, a keen understanding of every country's red lines, and a sensitivity to the shifting sands of political allegiances as governments changed. The role demanded a delicate balancing act—one where building consensus among conflicting interests was both a science and an art.

However, I was struck by how many elements were familiar to me yet intertwined with a host of new challenges. My seven years at NITI Aayog and my time as Secretary, DPIIT, had equipped me with a solid understanding of the priorities that would shape our work—be it the Sustainable Development Goals (SDGs), climate action, or digital transformation initiatives. These were staples of my prior experience, grounding me amidst the whirlwind of preparations for the G20 presidency.

With India's presidency beginning just a few months later, in December, I was also inheriting the role three-quarters of the way through Indonesia's term, which meant I had to pivot quickly, learning to swim midstream so that the transition to our chairmanship was seamless.

By early 2023, close to sixty cities in India were abuzz with the news that G20 meetings would be held in their city. The G20 became a talking point amongst the local population. The question on everyone's mind was: What is G20? Why does it matter, and how does the G20 shape global policies? And what exactly does a Sherpa do?

The Genesis of G20

The Group of Twenty, or G20, is a forum that brings together the world's major economies. As of 2022, it accounted for 60 per cent of the world's population, 75 per cent of global trade, and 85 per cent of global gross domestic product (GDP).[1] With the inclusion of the African Union (AU) as a full-time member during India's presidency, these figures further elevated the G20's representative power. Its primary objective is to foster international economic cooperation, making it the most influential body globally when it comes to setting the agenda, nudging economic policies, and holding world leaders accountable for their commitments to sustainable and inclusive growth.

We must go back in time to understand the genesis of the G20 as we know it today. In the 1970s, the Group of Seven (G7) was set up, consisting of the advanced economies of the time: the United States of America (USA), Canada, the United Kingdom (UK), West Germany, France, Italy, and Japan.

As the world continued to globalize, Asian economies rose to prominence in the 1980s and '90s. China stands out as a notable example, but even economies such as Thailand and Malaysia exhibited impressive growth as global value chains (GVCs) started to take shape. This phenomenal growth was coming at a time when growth in advanced economies was slowing. Japan, for instance, entered its 'Lost Decade' in the '90s, a period of sluggish economic growth and recession.

As growth slowed in the advanced economies, increased investments flowed into Asia. These investments came in two forms: direct investments (such as building factories or businesses) and portfolio investments (like buying stocks and bonds). The influx of capital led to a surge in the Asian stock markets and a rapid increase in real estate prices, creating financial bubbles.

As exchange rates were pegged to the US dollar, exports remained competitive as long as the US dollar did not appreciate

---

[1]The Group of Twenty (G20), *india.gov.in*, https://tinyurl.com/3aws87sr. Accessed on 30 August 2024.

significantly. An easy money regime globally meant that domestically, credit was booming in these Asian economies. Corporations took on large loans, home loans became easy, and money flowed into the equity markets. These countries also increasingly ran current account deficits (CADs)—spending more than they earned from exports—and relied on foreign borrowing, both from governments and corporates, often through short-term loans. With lower interest rates abroad and a stable exchange rate, credit growth was also fuelled by foreign capital.

However, the economic troubles began when the advanced economies raised their interest rates. The US Federal Reserve, for instance, did something similar as the US recovered from a recession, raising interest rates. This made investing in the US more attractive, prompting investors to pull their money out of Asian economies and invest back into the US.

The Asian economies, which were already struggling with high prices and overvalued currencies, felt the heat. They had to dip into their foreign exchange (forex) reserves to maintain their currency values. As these reserves dwindled, Thailand became the first country to devalue its currency, the Thai baht, in July 1997. This started a chain reaction. Malaysia, Indonesia, and the Philippines followed suit, devaluing their currencies too. South Korea faced a severe financial crisis, nearly defaulting on its debts.

Foreign investors pulled out money from these economies. Those who relied on foreign borrowing suffered a double whammy: Firstly, devalued currencies meant that they had to pay back more in their local money for every dollar borrowed. Secondly, these loans were based on interest rates in the advanced economies. As interest rates started rising, borrowers were faced with both interest rate risk and foreign exchange risk. Many went bankrupt. Banks were faced with mounting non-performing assets (NPAs). Both foreign funding and credit dried up.

These events collectively cascaded into the Asian Financial Crisis in 1997. Investment rates fell, jobs were lost, and inflation soared, pushing these countries into a deep recession. The shockwaves spread globally. In 1998, Russia experienced its own financial crisis. Following the dissolution of the Soviet Union in 1991, the Russian economy was heavily indebted. The expensive war in Chechnya came at a huge fiscal cost, resulting in the fiscal deficit ballooning. The Asian Financial Crisis reduced global demand for commodities and energy, hitting Russia hard. This caused its foreign currency reserves to fall. Rising debt, along with rising imports and speculative currency attacks, forced Russia to devalue the rouble. The country defaulted on its domestic debt and had to declare a moratorium on foreign debt payments.

In the same year, the effects were felt in the US when a highly leveraged, prominent hedge fund, Long Term Capital Management (LTCM), collapsed due to exposure to both the Asian Financial Crisis and the Russian Financial Crisis.

Amidst a continuous series of failures, the international financial architecture established post-World War II was unable to contain the crisis. The response of the G7 along with the International Monetary Fund (IMF) was seen as inadequate at a time of increasingly globalized and interdependent financial flows. A platform that represented both the developed and developing world was needed. Experience with the Asian Financial Crisis demonstrated that cooperation amongst the developed and developing world was essential to maintain international financial stability. In September 1999, the G20 forum was born, at the meeting of the G7 Finance Ministers and Central Bank Governors in Washington DC. It comprised the Finance Ministers and Central Bank Governors from twenty countries. Initiated by the Finance Minister and later Prime Minister of Canada Paul Martin along with Lawrence Summers, then US Secretary of the Treasury, the

G20 was established '*as a new mechanism for informal dialogue in the framework of the Bretton Woods institutional system, to broaden the dialogue on key economic and financial policy issues among systemically significant economies and to promote cooperation to achieve stable and sustainable world growth that benefits all.*'[2]

Amidst this backdrop of economic volatility and global interconnectedness, the G20 emerged as a crucial platform for navigating financial stability and policy coordination on a global scale, a role that would be put to the test less than a decade later in 2008, when the world faced another major upheaval. Amid peak globalization, what began as a 'credit crunch' in 2007 spiralled into the Global Financial Crisis (GFC) a year later. When Lehman Brothers collapsed in September 2008, the world was staring down the barrel of a deep recession yet again. Only this time it would be one of the worst since the Great Depression of the late 1920s.

Much has been written about the causes of the GFC. In a nutshell, the story is the same—asset bubbles that eventually burst. However, it is also a story of financial regulation gone wrong, poor credit policies, overreliance on rating agencies and, quite simply, irrational exuberance. As usual, the industry, academia, regulators, and the international financial architecture did not see this coming.

The GFC was a crisis of unprecedented proportions. Banks and financial institutions collapsed. Economic ramifications spread like wildfire across the globe, including India, where the Bombay Stock Exchange (BSE) Sensex, which stood at over 21,000 points in January 2008, fell to 8,000 points by the end of 2008, wiping out more than 50 per cent of the market value.[3]

---

[2]G20 Information Centre, *University of Toronto*, https://tinyurl.com/mwpe729w. Accessed on 30 August 2024.

[3]'Biggest falls in Indian stock market history', *Rediff*, 24 October 2008, https://tinyurl.com/mww2as7v. Accessed on 30 August 2024.

The GFC saw the genesis of the G20 in its current form. Realizing the gravity of the crisis, the meeting of Finance Ministers was elevated to the leaders' level.

At the time, I had just wrapped up my role as Joint Secretary in the Ministry of Tourism. Having recently stepped away from a position focused on promoting India as a prime travel destination, I watched with concern as the crisis took its toll on tourism and investments. The downturn was palpable, travel bookings plummeted, and the once-bustling industry faced overwhelming challenges. Businesses in the hospitality sector struggled to stay afloat and the economic repercussions were being felt across the board. Companies faced significant challenges in attracting the foreign investments they desperately relied upon. Those of us who had worked to support India's burgeoning tourism sector, pouring effort into marketing campaigns and partnerships, struggled to see that hard work threatened by a wave of economic uncertainty.

During this tumultuous time, the Indian government felt a sense of policy paralysis. With economic uncertainty hanging over us, decision-making became sluggish, hampering our ability to respond effectively. Observing from afar, I realized the crisis brought to light a crucial lesson—our governance model needed to evolve. We required a system that could deliver quick and effective solutions, especially in the face of unexpected adversity.

The events of this period reinforced my understanding of how global crises disproportionately impact the Global South, leaving emerging economies scrambling to regain their footing. It became evident that the existing global economic architecture, which heavily favoured developed countries, was not conducive to addressing the needs of developing nations during such critical moments.

This realization was reinforced during my time at NITI Aayog, where I engaged with a variety of economic issues that highlighted the vulnerabilities of the Global South. In numerous discussions and policy formulations, it became starkly clear how global crises, such as economic downturns or public health emergencies, often left developing nations at a disadvantage. Our analytical work revealed that the structures in place—designed primarily by and for the interests of developed countries—failed to provide adequate support or resources for those of us in emerging economies.

The 2008 GFC was the first major economic upheaval since the Asian Financial Crisis of the late 1990s. This time, however, it was evident that the lessons learnt from previous crises were critical. Armed with the understanding that a collective response was the key to navigating the challenges posed by the Asian Financial Crisis, world leaders were faced with the urgency of addressing this new threat. At this eye-opening juncture in economic history, then US President George W. Bush recognized that the fallout from the financial turmoil extended beyond borders, eroding wealth and destabilizing economies globally. He asserted that only the Heads of State could effectively tackle this crisis, highlighting the need for coordinated action at the highest level.

The first G20 Leaders' Summit was held in 2008 in Washington DC. In April 2009, during the second G20 Summit in London, leaders came together to address the escalating GFC. This crucial gathering set the stage for discussions that would shape international economic policy. Later that year in September, the third summit was held in Pittsburgh, where leaders designated the G20 as the 'premier forum for international economic cooperation.'[4] From this point onwards, the summit meetings were held semi-annually until 2010 and annually from 2011.

▪

[4]'What is the G20 Summit?' *Ministry of Foreign Affairs Japan*, https://tinyurl.com/363u5jd7. Accessed on 30 August 2024.

The G20 is unique for several reasons. It serves as a compass, providing guidance and proposals on global economic, social and developmental issues to member countries, international organizations (IOs), forums and global markets.

Unlike traditional bodies, there is no permanent secretariat or headquarters for the G20. Each member country takes turns assuming the presidency, staffing the secretariat, and shaping the agenda for the year. The presidency rotates annually, ensuring various voices are heard and adapting to current challenges. Each presidency has the liberty to invite selected countries and IOs to partake in the proceedings for the year.

An internal grouping called the Troika comprising the preceding, current and next presidency exists to provide continuity to the G20 agenda. Compared to other multilateral institutions, there is no voting in G20. Designed as a forum for deliberation rather than decision-making, the G20 issues declarations only with a full consensus among all members. The Sherpa is to negotiate between competing and complementary country interests and ultimately forge this unanimous consensus.

The G20 operates through two primary tracks: the Sherpa Track and the Finance Track. Each grouping holds discussions based on the subject.

The Sherpa Track currently hosts fourteen working groups (WGs), a number that has seen considerable growth over the years. As depicted in the table below, this evolution highlights a transformative shift in the G20's priorities. What began as a forum primarily devoted to financial issues has gradually expanded to adopt a 'whole of economy' approach, acknowledging the interconnected nature of global challenges and the necessity for holistic solutions.

TABLE 1
Sherpa Track Working Groups

No.	Working Group	Established
1	Agriculture	2011
2	Anti-Corruption	2010
3	Culture	2020
4	Development	2010
5	Digital Economy	2021
6	Disaster Risk Reduction*	2023
7	Education	2018
8	Employment	2014
9	Energy Transition**	2013
10	Environment and Climate Sustainability**	2013
11	Health	2017
12	Tourism	2020
13	Trade and Investment	2016
14	Women Empowerment	2023

*Established during India's presidency
**The Energy and Sustainability Working Group was de-linked in 2018, with Energy Transition and Environment & Climate becoming separate WGs.

The Development Working Group (DWG), the oldest working group within the G20, stewards its development agenda. During India's presidency, the DWG was the only WG housed in the same building as the G20 Secretariat, making our collaboration second nature. I remember daily exchanges on developmental issues, be it over impromptu coffee meetings or marathon planning sessions, where we charted India's development priorities and came up with strategies for negotiations. The DWG also acts as a crucial nodal body that liaised with relevant ministries—such as the Ministry of Agriculture and Farmers' Welfare for the Agriculture Working Group, or the Ministry of Electronics and Information Technology (MeitY) for the Digital Economy Working Group, and so forth—to ensure our development goals were holistically integrated and effectively advanced. With the fundamental interdisciplinary nature of development, blending expertise from various sectors was essential to ensure a cohesive strategy.

The G20 established the Agriculture Working Group in the wake of global food price volatility in 2011, in recognition of the urgent need for a coordinated response to agricultural challenges. Following closely, in 2014, a dedicated group focused on employment was formed, echoing the G20's commitment to fostering job creation amid shifting economic landscapes. By 2016, the establishment of the Trade and Investment Working Group further showed the G20's adaptability. Initially, discussions on energy and climate were intertwined in 2013, a crucial step that marked a turning point in recognizing the interconnectedness of these domains. However, in a move towards more targeted dialogue, Argentina's presidency in 2018 led to their separation.

The G20 has continued to evolve, with recent expansions resulting in new working groups dedicated to the digital economy, culture and tourism. Under India's presidency, we took a significant step forward by introducing the Disaster Risk Reduction (DRR) group and agreeing to establish a working group focused on women's empowerment. This ongoing evolution reflects how the G20 adapts its agenda in response to global crises and emerging trends while remaining committed to addressing the pressing issues facing our member nations.

Unlike the Sherpa Track, where WGs, each with multiple chairs, are driven by the host country, the Finance Track has other assigned leadership that takes its agenda forward. The Finance Track is headed by Finance Ministers and Central Bank Governors, who meet four times a year, with two meetings coinciding with the annual World Bank–IMF meetings. The host country plays a relatively limited role in the Finance Track compared to the Sherpa Track. However, despite the limited role in the Finance Track, India was able to push through transformative outcomes, owing to the leadership of Finance Minister Nirmala Sitharaman and Reserve Bank of India Governor, Shaktikanta Das.

TABLE 2

Finance Track Working Groups
Framework
International Financial Architecture
Infrastructure
Sustainable Finance
Global Partnership for Financial Inclusion
Joint Finance and Health Taskforce

Within the G20 framework, the presidency identifies key priorities and drafts comprehensive issue notes for each WG. These notes outline the challenges at hand, identify constraints, and propose potential solutions. They serve as the foundation for the year's deliberations.

During India's presidency, each WG convened four times throughout the year, culminating in ministerial meetings that finalized the work of these groups. The outcome of each meeting was typically a joint declaration or communique, which had to be endorsed by the relevant line ministers. Only if all ministers agree unanimously can the document be categorized as a declaration or a communique. If even one minister expresses dissent, the document is instead referred to as a Chair's Summary and Outcome Document (CSOD). This was the case for both Indonesia and India, which had to publish CSODs for working groups because of a lack of consensus on geopolitical paragraphs relating to the Russia-Ukraine conflict.

Apart from the Sherpa and Finance Tracks, the G20 also comprises several Engagement Groups (EGs) which represent civil society participants in the G20 process. Their recommendations are often considered for inclusion in the Leaders' Declaration. During our presidency, we added the Startup20 Engagement Group to the mix, reflecting the voice of innovators and entrepreneurs in the G20 agenda.

CHART 1

G20 Engagement Groups

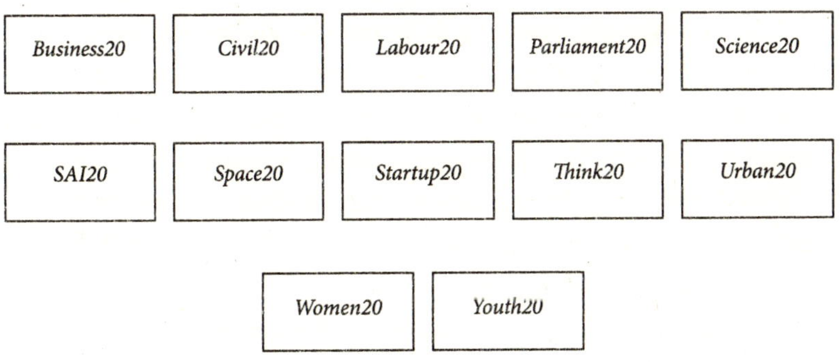

Transformative Presidencies

Strong political drive from the leaders characterizes the most successful presidencies, complemented by relevant content that inspires action. Several G20 presidencies have produced major success stories that left lasting imprints on the global stage—whether through direct measures or by initiating new work streams that resonated long after their tenure. The 2008 Summit in Washington DC and the 2009 Summit in London, for instance, were decisive moments. They orchestrated the G20's coordinated response to the GFC, breathing stability back into the world economy. One of the significant outcomes was the creation of the Financial Stability Board (FSB) from the Financial Stability Forum. This was a monumental addition to the global financial architecture, the first since the creation of the Bretton Woods Institutions post-World War II.

The 2008 financial crisis had cast a dark shadow over the global economy, leaving leaders grappling for solutions. In their first display of unity, the G20 leaders agreed not to resort to protectionism. This commitment was vital at a time when the vulnerabilities of globalization were coming to light, as it reassured a world teetering on the brink of economic collapse that countries would stand together to revive global trade and foster growth.

In those early years, stabilizing the global economy was paramount. By 2010, as leaders gathered in Toronto, the focus had shifted to sovereign debt—a looming spectre threatening the nascent recovery. The developed nations, burdened by crippling deficits and skyrocketing borrowing, pledged to rein in their debts. The decisions made in Toronto set the stage for a more disciplined financial approach.

Later that same year, in Seoul, the G20 took another significant step forward. The adoption of Basel III norms brought stricter capital and liquidity requirements for banks, a direct response to the reckless financial practices that had fuelled the crisis.[5]

---

[5]Basel III is an internationally agreed set of measures developed by the Basel Committee on Banking Supervision in response to the financial crisis of 2007–09. The measures aim to strengthen the regulation, supervision and risk management of banks. Basel III standards are minimum requirements which apply to internationally active banks.

Moreover, a reform of voting shares within the IMF was agreed upon, signalling a shift towards a more equitable and representative global financial system. This was also a transformative year for the G20 as it established the Development and Anti-Corruption working groups, expanding its focus beyond financial stability to long-term development and integrity.

In 2011, the G20 launched the Agricultural Market Information System (AMIS) under France's presidency. This initiative came at a critical time when global food prices were volatile, and food security was a pressing concern. The following year, Mexico's presidency saw a firm commitment to finalizing the IMF quota review process, further cementing the G20's influence on global financial governance.

The momentum continued to build. In 2014, leaders gathered in Brisbane adopted a bold initiative—the Brisbane 25 by 25 goal, aimed at reducing the gender gap in the labour force by 25 per cent by 2025. This marked a significant stride towards gender equality.

2015 was a turning point, as the G20 addressed the harrowing reality of the refugee crisis for the first time. The world watched in horror as over a million people fled conflict-ridden areas in West Asia, seeking safety and a new beginning. This human tragedy accentuated the necessity for collective action.

Under China's presidency in 2016, the G20 nations embraced the G20 Action Plan on the 2030 Agenda for Sustainable Development. This comprehensive plan was a guiding star, steering the G20's efforts to achieve the SDGs, which had been introduced just a year prior.

However, not all G20 summits have been smooth sailing. By 2017, the world was grappling with new threats. Germany's presidency marked the first significant discussion on terrorism at the G20, set against the backdrop of the 2015 Paris Climate

Agreement and the contentious decision by the US to withdraw from it during Donald Trump's presidency. Despite this setback, the G20 countries stood firm, reaffirming the 'irreversibility' of the Paris Agreement and directed multilateral development banks (MDBs) to promote access to affordable and clean energy. The United States' perspective on climate was incorporated in the main text of the paragraph rather than in a footnote. This would later give us the precedence we needed in the G20 to reflect diverse views in the main text, rather than as footnotes. At the 2018 Osaka Summit in Japan, the Sherpas themselves were unable to agree by the time the leaders arrived. It was only with the last-minute intervention of leaders that a declaration could be concluded.

The year 2020 brought the world to its knees with the onset of the COVID-19 pandemic. Saudi Arabia's presidency responded with decisive action, suspending government debt repayments for the world's poorest nations to alleviate the recession's unprecedented strain. This compassionate move illustrated the G20's ability to adapt and respond to crises with solidarity and resolve.

From steering the world through financial calamities to addressing social inequalities and environmental imperatives, the G20's elevation to the leader level has indelibly shaped the global agenda. Each presidency has responded to the needs of the time, and when it was India's turn to steer the ship, nothing less was expected. However, the circumstances surrounding India's presidency were fraught with numerous challenges, starting with COVID-19 in 2020.

Confronting Interconnected Crises

The COVID-19 pandemic saw millions of lives lost globally. According to World Health Organization (WHO) estimates, more than 750 million people were infected globally, with close to seven million deaths by December 2023.[6] Health systems around the world buckled under pressure when the pandemic was at its peak, exposing a glaring lack of investments in healthcare infrastructure, insurance, and coverage nets. The economic toll was equally devastating. Millions of jobs were lost as countries descended into a deep recession. The International Labour Organization (ILO) reported that by September 2020, the estimated loss of working hours equalled 495 million full-time equivalent (FTE) jobs globally.[7] This meant that the combined effect of lockdowns, transportation disruptions, and illness resulted in an unprecedented three-month loss of work, equivalent to nearly half a billion full-time jobs.

The pandemic was a real setback for the 2030 Agenda. The UN Sustainable Development Goals 2022 report stated that more than four years of progress in the fight against poverty was reversed by COVID-19. Education faced severe disruption, and learning outcomes suffered a severe setback across the world. The report stated that close to 147 million children globally missed more than 50 per cent of their in-person instruction during the COVID-19 years. The report also estimated that as many as 24 million children would potentially not return to learning.[8] G20 leaders would recognize in the New Delhi Leaders' Declaration that just 12 per cent of the SDG targets were on track in 2023.

The pandemic and its aftermath starkly illustrated the pervasive inequalities in our world. Developed countries could afford both extensive fiscal stimuli and large-scale vaccine procurement, tapping

---

[6]World Health Organization, *COVID-19 epidemiological update, 22 December 2023*, https://tinyurl.com/5y4v662n. Accessed on 4 September 2024.

[7]International Labour Organization,*ILO Monitor: COVID-19 and the world of work. Sixth edition*, 23 September 2020, https://tinyurl.com/4d7ay4u8. Accessed on 4 September 2024.

[8]Sustainable Development Goals, *The Sustainable Development Goals Report 2022*, 7 July 2022, https://tinyurl.com/5n9ak8ct. Accessed on 4 September 2024.

into financial markets and increasing their borrowing and deficits to combat the crisis. In contrast, lower-income nations were left struggling. An ILO report in October 2021 highlighted this disparity: while high-income countries achieved 60 per cent vaccine coverage by October 2021, the figure for low-income countries was less than 5 per cent. In middle- and higher-income countries, the vaccination coverage rate was 15 per cent and over 50 per cent, respectively. Regionally, Africa had the lowest vaccination rate at around 5 per cent, compared to 50 per cent in Europe, Central Asia, and the Americas.[9] Countries that could afford these fiscal measures, including India, saw stronger recoveries.

This disparity has defined the contours of the world for generations. Even before the multiple economic shocks of the past few years, low-income and developing countries accessed finance at rates 5 to 8 per cent higher than their developed counterparts.[10] As their capital markets are still underdeveloped, these countries often resort to external markets for financing.

During the pandemic years of 2020–22, central banks globally cut interest rates to infuse liquidity into the markets, allowing some countries to borrow at lower interest rates. Exchange rates had also largely stabilized by this point, providing fragile comfort amid the chaos.

But this was not to last. The war in Ukraine had global ramifications. A crisis in food, fuel and fertilizers quickly ensued. Western Europe, grappling with its dependence on Russian energy imports, began the difficult process of extricating itself from this trade dynamic. The effect of this was immediate—global fossil-fuel prices ballooned.

---

[9]Ibid., p. 13

[10]United Nations, *United Nations Secretary-General's SDG Stimulus to Deliver Agenda 2030*, February 2023, https://tinyurl.com/yea4jbkz. Accessed on 3 October 2024.

Ukraine, a major exporter of grain, and Russia, a key supplier of fertilizers, saw their production and distribution severely disrupted. Therefore, food prices surged worldwide, hitting low-income countries the hardest and pushing already stretched household budgets past their breaking point. In high-income countries, inflation rose to a decade high.

It wasn't just geopolitics that fuelled inflation in these countries. In response to previous crises, the developed world stimulated their economies by putting money directly into people's hands through tax cuts or direct transfers. This injection of disposable income spurred immediate consumption, creating a fleeting sense of economic buoyancy. Yet, this spike in demand also led to rising prices.

This was compounded by other global disruptions—the semiconductor shortage and the 2021 Ever Given incident, where a massive container ship became lodged in the Suez Canal, blocking one of the world's most critical shipping routes for several days. This caused significant interruptions in global supply chains and shipping routes. These factors collectively stoked the inflationary fires.

Central banks around the world responded to this runaway inflation in a typical manner: by hiking interest rates significantly. For nations with large external debts—debt owed to foreign governments, banks, and multilateral institutions—this was catastrophic. Their debts, often denominated in foreign currencies like the US dollar, caused their repayment burdens to grow when interest rates in the US rose. Higher interest rates in wealthy nations cause capital to flow back into these safe havens, leaving low-income countries with depreciating currencies. The cost of repaying each dollar borrowed surged as their local currencies weakened. Nations like Sri Lanka and Pakistan found themselves ensnared in this economic vice, reminiscent of India's pre-1991 crisis.

The global chasm in wealth grew ever deeper. The world's most vulnerable countries found themselves in grave debt distress. By February 2023, over half of the world's poor lived in 52 debt-ridden countries facing the possibility of total economic collapse. A cost-of-living crisis affected 121 countries, pushing millions more into poverty. For these struggling economies to grow, they needed breathing room—space to stabilize and support to build resilience.

However, this growth had to differ from the industrial booms of the past.

Developing countries do not have the luxury of adopting the models pursued by the developed world and carbonize at the rates they once did. The rulebook has changed, and the stakes are now existential. The world is already dealing with a 1.1°C rise in temperature. Previously, it was expected that global warming would hit 1.5°C between 2030 and 2052, but we have already crossed that threshold in 2023. 2023 has been the hottest year since humans started recording temperatures 175 years ago. And 22 July 2024 has been the hottest in history. Even if all nationally determined contributions (NDCs) are met, we still risk surpassing the 2°C mark.[11] Failure to meet these collective NDCs puts us on the brink of breaching the 3°C mark. At these levels of warming, scientists predict the world could pass several catastrophic points of no return—crop yields will fall, diseases will spread, and rising seas will engulf coastal cities.

Natural disasters such as earthquakes, floods, hurricanes and wildfires are already wreaking havoc, and climate change promises to amplify their frequency and intensity. Between 2015 and

[11]Nationally determined contributions, or NDCs, are countries' self-defined national climate pledges under the Paris Agreement, detailing what they will do to help meet the global goal to pursue 1.5°C, adapt to climate impacts, and ensure sufficient finance to support these efforts.

2020, the world saw approximately 10 million hectares of forests vanish every year. Our marine ecosystems have fared no better, with more than two-thirds suffering damage, degradation and irreversible change. The 'global stocktake' at the 28th Conference of the Parties (COP) in UAE in 2023 sounded the alarm louder than ever.[12] What's at stake extends far beyond the economy. It's now a question of the very future of human civilization.

Despite not being the historical drivers of climate change, today's developing countries bear the brunt of its impacts. Most of the cumulative emissions can be traced back to now-developed nations, and per capita emissions in developing countries remain a fraction of those in wealthier nations. Yet, it's these nations that find themselves on the frontline of climate impacts. Island states face existential threats from rising sea levels as severe flooding devastates lives and livelihoods, and public health emergencies become more frequent. The future of food productivity is jeopardized by extreme temperatures and erratic rainfall, which will push more people into poverty and drive up food costs. Failure to act now risks erasing decades of developmental gains.

Acknowledging the principle of common but differentiated responsibilities (CBDR) isn't enough if commitments aren't met. At the 2009 United Nations Climate Change Conference, commonly called the Copenhagen Summit, developed countries pledged to mobilize $100 billion annually for climate finance—a goal they claimed to have reached in 2023.

Many analysts are of the view that this is a case of greenwashing—a term used to describe the practice of conveying a false impression of environmental responsibility. Greenwashing occurs when an entity spends more time and money marketing itself as environmentally friendly than minimizing its ecological

---

[12]United Nations Climate Change, 'Global Stocktake', https://tinyurl.com/m75xd3bh. Accessed on 4 September 2024.

impact. This can involve misleading claims, superficial initiatives, or projects that do not deliver meaningful benefits to the environment. For instance, a new coal power plant in Bangladesh counts as climate finance, as it is claimed that emissions are lower than older-generation coal plants. On the other extreme, it has been reported that Italy is financing the opening of gelato stores across Asia, and the US is financing a hotel expansion in Haiti—all have been termed as climate finance.[13]

Yet, experts highlight that trillions of dollars are required annually to effectively address climate and development challenges. Additionally, technology transfers are crucial for adaptation and mitigation but often become contentious issues in international negotiations, leaving developing countries without the resources or technology they need. The reality is clear: the inequities of the past persist, and the burden falls disproportionately on those least responsible for the crisis.

This imbalance—where the developing world, or the 'Global South', endures hardships it didn't create—reflects a skewed international order. We saw it during the pandemic, witnessed it in the pursuit of SDGs, and now face it acutely with climate change. As policymakers in India and around the globe grapple with these interconnected crises, the imperative for transformative change is undeniable. The path forward demands collective resolve for a profound reimagining of international solidarity and fairness.

Failure of the Multilateral System

Yet another challenge that confronted India as it took over the G20 presidency was the way multilateralism was floundering. Experts

[13]Rumney Emma, et al., 'Rich nations say they're spending billions to fight climate change. Some money is going to strange places', *Reuters*, 1 June 2023, https://tinyurl.com/ys94cu7h. Accessed on 4 September 2024.

attribute this failure to the origins of these institutions—designed to serve the interests of their primary funders, the dominant economies of the mid-20th century.

In the aftermath of World War II, the world lay in ruins, grappling with the realities of war that had shattered nations and devastated economies. Out of the ashes of this unprecedented devastation, world leaders sought to construct a new order premised on multilateral cooperation, one that would prevent future conflicts and promote lasting peace and stability. As PM Modi would later reflect, these global frameworks were premised on the belief that humanity had learnt its lesson—that the era of war was over.

Foremost among the new institutions were the UN, emerging from the failed League of Nations, and the Bretton Woods institutions—the IMF and the World Bank. These entities aimed to foster international economic cooperation, stability and development. Several other international organizations emerged as specialized agencies of the UN, such as WHO and Food and Agriculture Organization (FAO), among others. These institutions laid the foundation for the post-war order, guiding the global socio-economic policies for decades. Yet, these organizations were largely made by the West for the West, tunnel-visioned on the immediate impacts of the war on their territories, while largely ignoring or sidelining the rest of the world.

During the world wars, millions of soldiers from the colonies in Asia and Africa stepped forward to serve, with India providing 1.5 million troops in World War I and 2.5 million in World War II. India lost 112,747 soldiers in World War I and around 36,094 in World War II. Their contributions were undocumented and unheard in the annals of Western-centric histories. These countries, still reeling under colonial rule, had no seat at the table when these international organizations were formed. While these institutions served well in the immediate post-war era, they are increasingly seen as inadequate to address today's multifaceted challenges. The second era of globalization saw economies in Asia transformed. Trade flourished, and GVCs began to take shape.

Episodes of sovereign debt crises are becoming more frequent, exacerbated by the conditionalities and penal interest rates imposed by lenders. The Washington Consensus, which emphasizes free trade and deregulation, often fails to consider the nuanced needs of developing economies.[14] India's own experience during the 1991 IMF bailout bears proof of this complexity.

The existing geopolitical challenges further ripple through the international financial order, prompting deep economic recessions. These crises underline the urgency for a new mandate for international financial institutions and MDBs. The trillions of dollars required annually for achieving SDGs and climate targets in developing nations call for expanded MDB lending. With hundreds of trillions in public and private assets globally, leveraging these funds for SDG and climate projects could mitigate the funding gap. However, this necessitates creating secure and stable investment environments to attract private capital to these critical areas.

There is certainly an argument to be made that Washington Consensus policies have done more harm than good in low-income countries. The role of the IMF in managing and flagging risks in the global financial order has increasingly been called into question. The spillover of national financial crises to the regional and global levels is a major criticism. In turn, these crises caused deep economic recessions. Open capital markets, especially in

[14]The Washington Consensus is a list of policies that had gained support among Latin American policymakers in response to the macroeconomic turbulence and debt crisis of the early to mid-1980s.

small and low-income countries, can lead to immense volatility, and yet the IMF advocates for more.[15]

Once these countries do end up in distress, the number-one policy suggestion by the IMF is to instill austerity measures—i.e., massive cuts in government spending. While unproductive spending should be cut, what often happens is that capex or infrastructure investments come to a standstill as well. This leads to a deepening of the crisis. Even as a lender of last resort, IMF lending comes with onerous terms, keeping countries indebted and sometimes even transferring private debt onto public books. While the IMF has proven that it can act decisively, as reflected in the $15 billion aid package for Ukraine, at the same time Sri Lanka was made to wait more than a year for a fraction of this amount. Even during the European Debt Crisis of 2012, insolvent countries such as Portugal, Ireland and Greece received massive bailouts, many times their IMF quotas.

The security front also portrays the faltering multilateral order. Decades of stalemates and veto power manipulations at the United Nations Security Council (UNSC)—exemplified by the enduring conflict in Ukraine and numerous other crises—have rendered these bodies ineffective. Informal groupings like the G7, the BRICS, the Quad, and the Shanghai Cooperation Organization (SCO) have gained prominence, as consensus is more manageable within these smaller factions. The G20, encompassing both developed and developing nations, holds particular significance due to its influence on global population, trade, GDP and emissions. And within the G20, India has truly come of age as a member.

---

[15]Chibber, Ajay, 'Where in the world is the IMF?', *Business Standard*, 28 March, https://tinyurl.com/ye5sj89a. Accessed on 4 September 2024.

India on the World Stage

Looking back at India's international standing before the turn of the millennium, it's striking to consider how far we have come. For today's younger generation, much of India's prominence in global affairs may seem like an inevitability, something to be taken for granted. They often don't grasp the profound shifts that were necessary to reshape our national narrative. For many non-resident Indians (NRIs), the current pride in India's achievements stems from a long history of hard-won progress and profound changes that have allowed us to claim our place among the world's influential nations.

In the past, India struggled with perceptions as a developing country, often seen as economically and politically stagnant. The need for substantial measures to change this narrative was evident. For instance, the Commonwealth Games hosted in 2010 highlighted both our ambitions and our challenges. While the event was intended to showcase India's rising capabilities, the reality was marred by infrastructure issues and corruption scandals that threatened to overshadow our achievements. Many venues were incomplete and financial mismanagement became a source of national embarrassment. These experiences pushed us to confront our limitations and encouraged India to urgently improve its global standing.

Taking the lead, PM Modi made massive diplomatic efforts that were instrumental in reshaping India's global narrative. His frequent visits abroad played a pivotal role in rekindling and fortifying partnerships and keeping the international community engaged with India. During each visit, the PM interacted with the Indian diaspora. As relations between India and various nations strengthened, awareness of India's standing grew—not just among government officials but also among the general populace, including the youth and NRIs.

In 2023, PM Modi undertook significant diplomatic trips that further reinforced India's position on the global stage. In June, he paid a high-profile state visit to the US, which included at least three meetings with US President Joe Biden, an address to the US Congress, and interactions with top Silicon Valley CEOs. This marked a crucial opportunity to strengthen relations with one of India's key partners. Additionally, he travelled to Australia and France, further enhancing India's engagement in the Indo-Pacific region and Europe.

These diplomatic efforts maintained existing alliances but were also aimed at building new connections. Notably, Saudi Crown Prince Mohammed bin Salman extended his G20 visit, transforming it into a state-level bilateral meeting. On the sidelines of India's G20 Summit, the most ambitious multinational and multiregional geoeconomic and geostrategic project was signed. The announcement of the India-Middle East-Europe Corridor (IMEC) is inspired by trading routes of old. The eight IMEC signatories account for about half of the world's economy, and 40 per cent of its population. Collaboration with nations underscored India's commitment to multilateralism and inclusive dialogue, reinforcing its standing as a significant player on the world stage.

Dr S. Jaishankar, India's External Affairs Minister (EAM), also played a pivotal role in this transformation, making foreign policy more relevant to the domestic audience. He visited numerous universities and colleges, articulating how foreign policy directly affects the lives of Indians. The notion that we as a nation are now global citizens had begun to take root. Even though I am not a career diplomat, the interest in foreign policy was palpable and growing.

When I spoke about the G20 at various universities, I was met with an enthusiastic response. The students showed a keen interest, asking insightful questions and engaging in vibrant discussions. Their eagerness to understand India's role on the global stage signified a shift in perspective—an awareness of our journey and a recognition of the groundwork that has enabled us to navigate today's complexities. India's path has been replete with challenges, but these have been eclipsed by our achievements. The narrative of India is no longer one of potential, but one of realization. As we navigate the future, we must remember where we came from, ensuring that the pride in our progress continues to resonate across generations.

It was this sense of pride that imbued our efforts when we were presented with the unique opportunity to stand out and assert our identity on the global stage. We made a conscious effort to give our presidency a distinctive 'flavour of India' and showcase our rich culture and vibrant democracy. Our approach was not just about hosting an event, but also about demonstrating our competence and integrity, proving that India could manage international engagements on a scale that surpassed mere perfection.

TWO

HEALING, HARMONY AND HOPE

For generations, views fixated on the scarcity of resources have led to competition and conflict, resulting in a zero-sum mindset where one's gain was posited to another's loss. Engaging with the prevailing worldviews had only set humanity back decades in its developmental progress. It was against the backdrop of this narrative of greed and confrontation, amid tremendous global upheaval, that India assumed the presidency of the G20 on 1 December 2022.

Prime Minister Modi did not want the presidency to be more of the same and sought to change the very bedrock of this thought system. He believed India should focus on healing our planet through sustainable lifestyles, promoting harmony by depoliticizing essential global supplies, and instilling hope in future generations through an honest dialogue on global security.

The PM envisioned India's G20 presidency as an opportunity to revitalize multilateralism. His perspective was that while the world may have many geographical boundaries and different political ideologies, all humans come from one cosmos. We hoped to catalyze a profound ideological shift, inviting the world to see itself not as a collection of competing individuals and nations, but as a unified collective with shared destinies. Our common challenges could only be addressed through collective action and collaboration. With a vision to transcend the traditional dividing lines between the First World and the Third World, India's leadership aimed to foster a more inclusive, interconnected, and resilient global approach.

As India embarked on this journey, it did so not just as a country, but as a microcosm of the world, whose incredible diversity reflects the global community. With its rich democratic traditions and a culture of collective decision-making, India was poised to lead the G20 with a vision that blended millions of free voices into a harmonious melody.

This momentous event heralded a new chapter in diplomacy, underpinned by an ambitious and transformative approach to global leadership. It was India's moment on the global stage, a moment to transform the narrative from confrontation to cooperation, from division to unity, and from despair to hope. The G20 presidency under India's leadership was to be a presidency of healing, harmony and hope.

Ethos of the Presidency

Home to one-sixth of humanity, India has a young, enterprising population ready to seize opportunities while remaining resilient to risks. Today, India is the world's fastest-growing major economy, achieving sustainable prosperity through consistent economic growth and inclusive development. In this era of digital technology, with its ability to connect and mobilize on an unprecedented scale, India's vision is to harness these tools not just for economic growth but also to build a more cohesive and compassionate world. India's approach to governance focuses on inclusivity and nurturing the potential of its youth, ensuring that even the most marginalized voices are heard and valued.

India has emerged as a hotspot of optimism for addressing the key challenges that define our times. The cornerstone of this narrative lies in its philosophies that offer guidance amid bleak global prospects.

Guided by the timeless teachings of Mahatma Gandhi on need versus greed, India envisioned a path to prosperity that transcended mere economic growth. Gandhi's philosophy emphasized living in harmony with the Earth and preserving the balance of nature. This vision underscored the belief that true prosperity must go hand in hand with sustainability, reflecting traditional values such as *dharma* (duty) and *ahimsa* (non-violence), which promote responsible and sustainable living.

To this end, our national goals have been aligned with these objectives for the better part of a decade. We connected every village in India to the electricity grid, ensuring that even the most remote communities can be connected to the modern world. We exceeded our target for non-fossil electricity capacity nine years ahead of schedule, setting a new standard for clean energy leadership. We co-founded the International Solar Alliance (ISA) in 2015, which has grown from 32 ratified members in 2018 to an impressive 99 members today, showcasing the power of international cooperation in promoting renewable energy. We launched the world's largest agricultural pump solarization programme, transforming the agriculture sector with sustainable energy. We embraced digital transformation, empowering millions through financial inclusion and technological advancements. We championed women-led development, ensuring that progress included every segment of society. We invested in sustainable infrastructure and laid the foundation for a resilient and forward-looking nation.

It was this essence that PM Modi wanted to capture in the theme of India's G20 presidency—*Vasudhaiva Kutumbakam*, which translates to 'One Earth, One Family, One Future.' This ancient Sanskrit phrase from the *Maha Upanishad* reflects the belief that the entire world is one family. It transcends mere tolerance and acceptance, urging a universal bond of kinship, compassion and understanding among all living beings. It envisioned a reality where the means to meet the basic needs of all people are available, in which humanity's survival no longer hinges on conflict, and where global challenges like climate change, terrorism and pandemics demand collective action and solidarity.

This deep-rooted philosophy views all living beings and inanimate objects as being composed of the same five elements—the *panch tatva* of earth, water, fire, air and space. The harmony between these elements is seen as crucial to our collective well-being, both physically and environmentally.

Embracing this ethos, India's G20 presidency was not just about economic or political agendas, but about promoting a universal sense of oneness.

अयंबन्धुरयंनेतिगणनालघुचेतसाम्
उदारचरितानांतुवसुधैवकुटुम्बकम्

(The distinction 'this person is mine, and this one is not' is made only by the narrow-minded. For those of noble conduct, the whole world is one family.)

This shift in ideology was also exemplified in real-world actions. India's external economic and development cooperation are in line with the SDGs and the principles of mutual respect, care for the future, and diversity. This cooperation is rooted in the belief that we can solve global issues if we work together as a cohesive unit and not as opposing factions.

India's rich heritage also played a crucial role in shaping our approach to the G20 presidency, where we sought to blend ancient wisdom with contemporary global challenges, offering unique perspectives and solutions. India's history of civilization, one of the oldest in the world, is replete with examples of scientific, mathematical, cultural and philosophical advancements. From the concept of zero to the philosophical depths of Vedanta, from architectural marvels like the Taj Mahal to modern technological advancements, India's journey has been one of continuous evolution, resilience, and inclusive growth.

On the first day of India's G20 presidency, a remarkable transformation unfolded across India's historical landmarks. In a symbolic gesture, one hundred centrally protected monuments, including several UNESCO World Heritage sites, were lit up simultaneously for seven days from 1 to 7 December.

The monuments that joined in this luminous tribute included the Red Fort in Delhi, the Royal Palace of Mandu and the Sanchi Stupa in Madhya Pradesh, Krishna's Butterball, the Thanjavur Big Temple in Tamil Nadu, and the historic site of Nalanda in Bihar, among others. This pan-Indian illumination was an intentional act of unity, meant to showcase the web of civilization that connects diverse regions and cultures under a shared history—diverse yet wholly Indian. As these monuments lit up, they told stories of India's past, present and future. They stood as sentinels not just of India's heritage but also of its commitment to play a pivotal role in shaping a balanced and inclusive world order.

Guiding Philosophy

'As India's ancient saying goes, the wise look at the world as one family,' PM Modi remarked in 2015.[1]

This push for a human-centred approach influenced every G20 decision. PM Modi's belief in fair progress resonated in our initiatives, fostering an inclusive environment where every nation, regardless of power, could thrive. This presidency became a real-life application of his ideals, enhancing collective responsibility and well-being.

The inaugural G20 meeting in November 2022 was the first visible manifestation of this approach, gathering ambassadors from 29 nations on the serene Andaman and Nicobar Islands. Choosing these breathtaking islands underscored our commitment to inclusivity, ensuring no part of India remained untouched by the G20's influence. The natural beauty of the Andamans reinforced

[1]Statement by Prime Minister Shri Narendra Modi at the Sustainable Development Summit New York, 25 September 2015, https://tinyurl.com/5d2abpp5. Accessed on 4 September 2024.

our theme of One Earth, One Family, One Future, representing India's global vision.

Set against this stunning backdrop, we shared India's perspectives and G20 plans, emphasizing our diverse priorities. The choice of location extended discussions beyond theoretical debates, drawing attention to climate change and vulnerable populations. This setting, amidst the Indian Ocean's expanse, highlighted the G20's tangible effects on fragile ecosystems like the Andaman and prompted a deeper appreciation of the consequences of global decisions.

For the delegates of the G20 countries, witnessing the beauty of the Andamans firsthand deepened their commitment to protecting our planet and people. The G20's engagement with the islands reaffirmed our dedication to engaging all sections of the nation in global dialogues, ensuring our decisions reflect the diversity and uniqueness of India.

The logo of India's G20 presidency, rich in symbolism and meaning, was also deeply embedded in the country's ethos and identity. Inspired by the vibrant colours of our national flag—saffron, white, green and blue—the logo was a harmonious juxtaposition of the Earth and the lotus, India's national flower. Rising from murky waters, the lotus symbolizes growth amid challenges, resilience, and the ability to stay untouched by the impurities of its surroundings—a fitting metaphor for the ideals India aimed to project in its G20 leadership. Beneath the logo, the word Bharat was inscribed in the Devanagari script, grounding the logo in India's linguistic heritage.

The logo was not just a visual symbol but also a narrative, conveying India's message of striving for just and equitable growth for all, navigating through turbulent times in a sustainable, holistic, responsible and inclusive manner. It represented a uniquely Indian approach to the G20 presidency, emphasizing living in harmony with the surrounding ecosystem.

As the G20 presidency progressed, the logo became ubiquitous, adorning highways, roads, buildings, and even the historical monuments of India. It transcended its official capacity, weaving itself into the fabric of everyday life. In cities and towns, street artists incorporated the logo in their graffiti, splashing walls with vibrant colours and creative interpretations, turning it into a symbol of pride and hope.

The logo design was the result of an open competition hosted on the MyGov portal, which saw over 2,000 submissions, reflecting the ethos of *Jan Bhagidari,* or public participation, a key theme in the PM's vision for the G20 presidency. This approach was not only symbolic of India's commitment to democratic values and inclusive governance, but it also ensured that the G20 presidency was a representation of the collective spirit and aspirations of people across India and the world.

A People-Centric Celebration

In a country known for its diversity, the spirit of *Atithi Devo Bhava* (the guest is God) permeates every corner of society, drawing from deep-rooted cultural and religious traditions. This ethos emphasizes hospitality and a sense of familial obligation towards others, creating a natural environment for nurturing connections and collaborations. As India geared up to assume the G20 presidency, this collective belief resonated in the preparations, embodying our commitment to inclusivity and warmth.

Further, PM Modi saw our G20 presidency as more than just high-profile meetings and envisioned it as an opportunity to democratize diplomacy and engage citizens, turning it into a 'people's presidency'. The aim was to decentralize conversations so that diverse regions of India had a stake in critical global policy discussions.

The pioneer was the state of Rajasthan, which hosted the first Sherpa meeting of the presidency in Udaipur on 4 December 2022. The state government transcended narrow political divisions and showed that the G20 was at its heart about unity and common goals.

This meeting also epitomized PM Modi's call to 'turn local into global' by embracing local art forms amidst Udaipur's stunning lakes and historic palaces. On the first day, the age-old *Jal Sanjhi* (water painting) art form mesmerized the audience. Renowned artist Rajesh Vaishnav brought this 300-year-old tradition of Rajasthan to life on the water, offering a fascinating insight into this rich artistic heritage. The event also featured millet snacks and Rajasthani *bandhani* bags—an attempt to share India's cultural wealth with the world.

The celebration continued with the Desert Music Symphony led by Sangeet Natak Akademi awardee Gazi Khan Barna. The performance celebrated the musical heritage of Rajasthan through the folk traditions of Langa and Manganiyar, featuring instruments like the *kamaicha*, Sindhi sarangi, and *morchang*, to name a few. Highlighting indigenous art forms and musical traditions served a dual purpose of showcasing the vibrant cultural fabric of India and sending a poignant message of preserving this precious heritage. These artistic expressions are integral to India's identity—being not just relics of the past but also vital threads in the nation's sense of self-determination.

Throughout the G20 presidency, over 300 cultural programmes featured an extraordinary array of local and national art forms, with the participation of over 20,000 local artists.

In Varanasi, 101 musicians from all over the world performed the *Sur Vasudha*—a fusion orchestral piece that saw a Brazilian conga play alongside an Indian mridangam at the end of the meeting of culture ministers. Scottish bagpipes joined the Indian shehnai, Italian violins harmonized with an Indian sarangi, and the English flute kept time with the *bansuri* (flute), all inspired by the sitar and French horn to seamlessly blend Western and Eastern musical traditions.

This was followed by the piece *Vasudhaiva Kutumbakam*. Vocalists representing their unique cultural heritage sang in 29 different languages, with visuals of smiling faces from around the world projected on a giant screen. This performance brought to life the concept of the world as one family, transcending linguistic barriers and celebrating the diversity and interconnectedness of humanity.

The G20 orchestra in Varanasi was a powerful symbol of India's vision of a united world. It demonstrated how music, a universal language, can bridge differences, connect hearts, and reinforce the message that despite our diverse backgrounds, we are all part of one global family.

The Bharat Yatra Musical Ensemble, conceptualized by the Sangeet Natak Akademi, was a highlight of the Gala Dinner of the G20 Leaders' Summit in New Delhi. The ensemble brought together an unprecedented variety of musical instruments and talent from across the country. Featuring 34 Hindustani instruments, 18 Carnatic instruments, and 23 folk instruments, it represented a microcosm of India's vast musical heritage. Over 75 artists, including children, women and *divyung* (differently abled) artists, created an unforgettable melody. Rare instruments like the *urdhak*, the *ravanhatta*, the *jal tarang* and the *pepa*, alongside traditional instruments like the *shehnai* and the sitar, created a mesmerizing musical journey that left the audience spellbound. The concept originated from the PM himself, who believed that the leaders, given their exhaustive schedules, would benefit more from an opportunity to network informally as the ensembles played in the background.

Collectively, events like these reached over 233 million participants, including students, teachers and community members.

Achieving such remarkable engagement was the result of cooperative federalism in action. This message was reinforced when PM Modi chaired the first virtual meeting of chief ministers and governors of all states on 9 December to discuss myriad aspects of the presidency. He clarified that the G20 was for the people and beyond party politics, and that all states and union territories must reflect this spirit. He particularly praised the Rajasthan government for its outstanding organization of the first Sherpa meeting in Udaipur.

During this session, Dr Jaishankar highlighted the significance and importance of hosting the G20 Summit. He emphasized that this was a unique opportunity for India.

I was tasked with presenting the significance of the G20 initiative from a bottom-up perspective. I highlighted that this could be a perfect moment for state leaders to capitalize on the momentum, leveraging the platform to foster grassroots development, enhance local economies, and usher in transformative change that resonated with the needs of their communities. Highlighting Rajasthan's impressive work in maintaining cleanliness, I recognized the collaborative efforts of its officials in supporting India's G20 vision. The Prime Minister encouraged other chief ministers to seize this moment to enhance their infrastructure, prioritize One District One Product (ODOP), and champion the use of millets.

The G20 needed to be a productive, not a disruptive, exercise for the cities that it touched. Right from our first meeting with the CMs and governors, we sought the support of the local administration to use this moment to showcase the best that India offers. This meant cleaning up and illuminating our archaeological sites properly, exhibiting the rich natural landscapes and architectural wonders of each state with its unique history.

This supported the local economy in the short term and boosted post-COVID tourism in the long term as it renewed interest in our wonders from tourists from around the world.

However, this meant that our presidency couldn't simply be relegated to talks behind closed doors. This was a golden opportunity to showcase the strength and unity of a country capable of bridging great divides.

But that was easier said than done. After all, India is anything but small. It's a country that stretches from arid deserts to lush rainforests within just a few hundred kilometres, a land where over a billion people speak hundreds of languages, each with its own colloquialisms and regional dialects. Crafting policy for such a diverse nation means creating frameworks that cater to a multitude of facets, addressing everything from urban tech hubs to remote agricultural communities.

Major sporting events like the Olympic Games take place in three to four major cities, spanning two to three weeks. Previous presidencies were restricted to a maximum of four to five cities. India's G20 presidency, in comparison, was held in 60 cities covering all states and union territories. We opened the doors of this elite summit to tier 2 and tier 3 cities, breaking new ground for inclusive governance.

The ambition of this effort within a tight timeline meant synchronizing a host of logistical elements across languages, terrain and weather—from transportation, accommodation and security to the cultural showcases and technical infrastructure required to support high-level international delegations.

It took meticulous coordination between ministries, local governments and international bodies to ensure each place, big or small, played a key role in India's global story. Each city had distinct cultural and infrastructural nuances. Engaging local stakeholders meant navigating different administrative processes, which tested the organizational skills of the entire team. However, this was an opportunity to illustrate not just India's capability to organize on a grand scale, but also its hospitality, innovation and identity, projecting the image of a nation ready to lead the world into a new era of cooperation and development.

We didn't want these cities to be just stagnant backdrops; each location was chosen for a reason. From the Deccan Plateau, the Deccan High-Level Principles on Food Security and Nutrition laid a robust foundation for addressing global challenges related to sustenance. In Chennai, the High-Level Principles for Blue/Ocean-based Economy echoed India's coastal identity, showcasing the nation's commitment to sustainable marine practices. The roadmap for tourism in Goa, inspired by this iconic destination, illustrated India's vision for a vibrant and responsible tourism sector. The Gandhinagar Implementation Roadmap for land restoration aligned with Gandhinagar's commitment to environmental sustainability, underscoring India's commitment to land stewardship. The Kashi Culture Pathway was the first time that the G20 members unanimously endorsed the advancement of culture as a standalone goal. Finally, the Jaipur Call for Action emphasized the enhancement of MSMEs, focusing on inclusive economic growth and empowerment. From Bengaluru's Digital Economy Ministerial Meet to Indore's 'zero waste' Employment Working Group event, each meeting highlighted regional diversity.

Cities like Jaipur, Varanasi, Srinagar and Nuh, and states like Goa, Tripura and Arunachal Pradesh became key players in shaping global agendas within the G20 framework, leaving an enduring legacy stamped with the identity of the place that inspired them. If we were to debate policies that affected local communities around the world, it was essential for us to immerse ourselves in these communities to witness firsthand civilizational practices that still maintain a symbiotic connection with nature and have drawn a thread into their past and future through their local customs.

The promotion of active stakeholder involvement and the encouragement of policy collaboration across states provided a unique opportunity to transform cities across the nation. For instance, the tourism landscape in Kashmir changed after the G20 Tourism Working Group meeting. The region recorded a significant uptick in visitors, with 15.65 lakh tourists in the first half of 2024 alone, an increase of 20 per cent over the previous year.[2] Lieutenant Governor Manoj Sinha also noted that the successful G20 meeting marked a turning point for tourism, as delegates returned home as enthusiastic ambassadors of the region, sharing stories of Kashmir's beauty and warmth. This revival was welcome news for many, including local entrepreneurs who saw a dramatic increase in their sales and bookings figures.

The improved security situation played a key role in this resurgence. Following the abrogation of Article 370 in 2019, the authorities made considerable efforts to enhance safety and appeal across Kashmir, showcasing their commitment to transforming the image of the valley. As I walked through the vibrant marketplaces of Srinagar, I observed delegates immersed in local life, haggling over pashmina shawls and savouring the flavour of authentic Kashmiri *kahwa*. It was a heartening sight to see representatives from over 20 countries appreciating what India had to offer, from the majestic Dal Lake to the intricately designed houseboats.

In New Delhi, we launched a massive campaign to ensure that the capital was ready to host the world. Much credit goes to the Principal Secretary to the PM, Dr P.K. Mishra, who constantly

---

[2]Hussain, Ashiq, 'Kashmir valley abuzz with tourists in first half of 2024, arrivals up 30%', *Hindustan Times*, 4 July 2024, https://tinyurl.com/3djw6stp. Accessed on 5 September 2024.

held inter-ministerial meetings and reviewed all preparations. The finalization of the venue for the leaders' meeting, Bharat Mandapam, posed some critical challenges. Always solution-oriented, he played a key role in ensuring the timely completion of the venue.

The Lieutenant Governor of Delhi, V.K. Saxena, a leader committed to the vision, pushed rapid implementation of beautification, cleanliness and greening on the ground. The Summit was the capital's grandest spectacle since the 2010 Commonwealth Games, eclipsing even the 1982 Asian Games and the 1983 NAM and CHOGM summits. Forty heads of state and numerous officials had to be welcomed amid tight security and an ongoing monsoon in one of the most densely populated cities in the world. Key areas, including Sardar Patel Marg and Shanti Path, were revamped, the roads adorned with 700,000 potted plants, and over a hundred statues and sculptures strategically placed. The streets were clean, and the visual clutter of political and commercial hoardings was absent.

Coordination between the various agencies was exceptional, covering 61 roads and 17 hotels to create a comfortable environment for the visiting delegations. The city's infrastructure was overhauled, and continuous efforts were made to maintain cleanliness and order. Public transport and daily life remained largely unaffected, demonstrating Delhi's capability to host significant international events seamlessly.

Saxena personally took me and Chief Coordinator Harsh Vardhan Shringla to Bansera Park, a place I had heard of but never imagined would be so imaginative. As we walked through the park, Saxena shared stories of its creation. Laid out in August 2022, Bansera Park is the city's first bamboo-themed park, sprawling over 10 hectares in the Yamuna floodplains. It was established with the G20 Summit in mind, and it showed.

The park is divided into two parts: bamboo recreation and bamboo plantation. It included different varieties of bamboo saplings, brought in from across the country. We walked past bamboo kiosks, huts, a watchtower, and seating areas, all a natural extension of the lush surroundings. The park's design was aimed at enhancing urban greenery and offering a refreshing outdoor space for the residents of Delhi.

The most striking feature was the air, noticeably fresher. Bamboo produces about 30 per cent more oxygen and consumes less water, which helps enrich the soil and combat air pollution. Nearby, a six-acre depression area was being transformed into a water body, adding to the park's atmosphere.

In Udaipur, we took on the ambitious task of cleaning Lake Pichola and restoring it to its original pristine beauty. In Kerala, the backwaters were revitalized and a new convention centre for the Sherpas was created. From lake clean-ups in Manipur and urban sanitation drives in Mumbai, to rapid infrastructure development in Lucknow, India saw significant improvements. Connectivity and accessibility have been improved through road repairs and the revitalization of public spaces, with parks and community centres emerging where neglected lots once stood. These efforts showcased India's commitment to ensuring that the G20 truly represented the needs of its people. Events like the International Kite Festival in Gujarat, the Hornbill Festival in Nagaland, and Model G20 sessions with schools in Bengaluru involved communities across the nation, demonstrating that high-level discussions must resonate with everyday realities.

The G20 presidency not only unified India but also involved every state, ensuring that local voices and concerns were incorporated into the global dialogue. The states worked overtime for almost a year to host spectacular G20 meetings, and PM Modi wanted to ensure that the outcomes of the G20 bore their unmistakable imprint.

▪

These stupendous efforts ensured the G20 Summit became a household name, achieving an unprecedented level of public engagement and awareness. We organized Jan Bhagidari events with a multi-faceted approach that seamlessly blended digital and physical activities. These initiatives aimed to raise awareness and encourage involvement across all segments of society. Over 233 million participants engaged in online discourse, while physical events—ranging from walkathons to flash mobs focused on women-led development and community leadership—were held at state, district, block, panchayat and school levels to ensure grassroots engagement. The scale of this involvement was unmatched; no other nation had ever witnessed such extensive participation in the G20 process.

Local events deepened the special features of the culture that make up India's identity. A prime example was the 'Saree Walkathon' in Surat, where 15,000 women from 15 states came together to celebrate India's rich textile heritage while promoting the Vocal for Local initiative. This vibrant event boosted Surat's textile industry and set the stage for local products to gain recognition on global platforms. The G20 Cyclothon rally, motorbike rally, and various urban development projects showcased the impact of physical initiatives in conveying transformative messages.

Families congregated around the G20 billboards, eagerly snapping selfies to immortalize the historic moments unfolding in their cities. School students embraced their creativity in interpreting global geopolitics through artistic endeavours, adding a youthful perspective to the discussions. A standout highlight of our inclusive approach was the G20 THINQ organized by the Indian Navy for students from all G20 nations. This initiative fostered global awareness among young minds and invited them to engage in international dialogues, enriching their understanding of world affairs. The finals of this quiz took place in November

2023 against the backdrop of India Gate, drawing participation from several countries.

Our strategy leveraged technology to transcend geographical limitations. The G20 University Connect lecture series reached students from Kochi to Karnal. Social media integration further ignited public engagement, leading to an astounding 14 trillion impressions—a clear sign of a well-executed digital communications plan.

This initiative didn't stop at the numbers. In Varanasi, the district administration set the world record for the highest number of participants in a quiz contest at multiple locations. Under the 'Culture Unites All' campaign led by the Ministry of Culture, the skills of over 450 Lambani women artisans from Sandur Kushala Kala Kendra were showcased with 1,755 items, setting a Guinness World Record. This achievement resonated with the PM's Lifestyle for Environment (LiFe) and the Culture Working Group's 'Culture for LiFe' initiatives, promoting sustainability and an eco-friendly lifestyle. Lambani embroidery, a traditional craft from Karnataka, is a tapestry of colours, mirror work, and diverse stitches, and shares similarities with textile traditions across Eastern Europe and Western and Central Asia, hinting at the historical movements of nomadic communities and a shared cross-border artistic culture. Choosing Lambani embroidery for this campaign was a masterstroke in cultural diplomacy. It underscored the concept of worldwide unity through art, celebrating India's cultural heritage and the shared histories that unite diverse communities worldwide.

Building a Cohesive Team

The G20, a confluence of global issues ranging from supply chain disruptions to the profound effects of climate change, necessitated expertise from a variety of fields. Given the scale of work needed to anchor 11 WGs under the Sherpa Track and an additional seven under the Finance Track, and several EGs with new leadership, G20 India, under the leadership of PM Modi, opted not to outsource the challenge to professional consultancy teams but instead build a robust internal team from scratch. The PM's vision extended beyond bureaucratic hierarchies, encouraging a culture where colleagues knew each other's strengths and weaknesses. Drawing parallels with the Swachh Bharat Abhiyan, he encouraged transforming projects into celebrations, fostering a collective spirit that transcended silos. This decision turned out to be strategically sound, as the youthful exuberance and willingness to tackle challenges head-on brought a fresh perspective to our work.

In response, we created special posts and actively recruited young professionals from different sectors including corporate, health, academia, policy, agriculture and energy, among others, so that we could approach each domain holistically to develop India's knowledge base. We also brought on deputation young officers from the armed forces to help plan the logistics. The precision and zeal with which they got their work done was impressive, to say the least. I also worked closely with the joint secretaries, a dynamic group composed not only of Indian Foreign Service (IFS) officers but also members of various All India Services. This marked my first significant collaboration with the Ministry of External Affairs (MEA) and the IFS. Working alongside these dedicated professionals opened my eyes to the nuances of international diplomacy and the importance of fostering cooperation. I quickly realized the value of our diverse perspectives coming together—combining the insights and implementation-oriented mindset of the Indian Administrative Service (IAS) representatives with the strategic thinking of the IFS created a robust atmosphere for dialogue and problem-solving.

It was clear that we needed to form a compact and efficient team, focusing not just on the substantive aspects, but also on the logistical intricacies involved in preparing for such a significant role. Collaboration would be key to our success.

However, in the early days, it took some time for us to find our rhythm and develop a common working language. However, initial friction gradually gave way to a cohesive understanding and teamwork, and we eventually made significant progress. The vibrant energy and diverse backgrounds of the team members enriched our discussions, creating an environment where lively debate and differing opinions were encouraged. We embraced the full spectrum of perspectives, realizing that only through constructive disagreement could we refine our ideas and make more informed decisions. Despite our varied viewpoints, we remained united by a common goal: to serve India and make it the most successful G20.

The G20 allowed everyone to break away from their traditional office routine and discover the abilities of their colleagues while working side by side. We embraced a cross-sector approach that broke down traditional departmental processes. Inclusivity was key, every voice was valued and considered. We walked the talk, practising the unity we preached.

This breaking of silos was possible because the tone was set from the top. PM Modi's outcome-oriented leadership style emphasized inclusive collaboration above all of us, inspiring us to unite our efforts towards a common goal. In asking nations to come together for the G20, PM Modi understood that we must lead by example at all levels, demonstrating the very unity we advocated on the global stage.

A culture of collaboration took root, driven by PM Modi's trust in our collective capabilities. The absence of silos encouraged professionals to support each other, pooling knowledge to represent the interests of a changing India—one that actively articulated the concerns of developing nations.

These chambers were broken internally within the government, but also outside of it. The Engagement Groups (EGs) evolved as important conduits that served as the voice of civil society. They acted as dynamic funnels, channelling expertise to the G20 deliberations and disseminating information and engagement back to the sectors they represented, fostering constant communication with stakeholders outside of government.

India's team was uniquely positioned to engage with the complexity of issues on the G20 agenda. It could negotiate effectively and undertake the necessary groundwork. Participating in the Indonesia-India-Brazil G20 Troika, the first led by emerging economies, showcased India's economic and political weight in reshaping the global narrative—and this responsibility was not taken lightly. Further, mapping each country's position during the meetings required a keen awareness of diplomatic nuances. Such was the task that success was only reserved for those willing to invest the time to do their homework, collaborate, and innovate relentlessly.

For India's G20 team, the Sushma Swaraj Bhawan became the nerve centre, a unique convergence point for substantive and logistical discussions. We met regularly, working together to tackle the myriad challenges that arose between the ministries and our EGs. The secretaries would frequently drop by to review our progress, eagerly enquiring about the status of negotiations and where we needed to apply additional pressure.

Consequently, each department had supervision—our priorities were fundamentally interconnected, and this fact shaped our collective endeavours. If one team fell behind in producing research or delivering essential information, it had a ripple effect on the overarching issues we were all focused on. The urgency of our mission meant that everyone felt the weight of responsibility—not just for their tasks, but also for the common goal of benefiting the global community. This sense of duty kept us all on our toes because we knew that our actions mattered far beyond our individual roles.

This constant communication allowed us to identify potential blockages within the line ministries early on, enabling us to prepare effectively for the Sherpa-level meetings.

Vibrant Cast of Characters

Each member of the team brought unique strengths and expertise to the table. Dr Jaishankar consistently pushed us to think beyond bureaucratic details and focus on achieving meaningful outcomes. His emphasis on delivery through constant reviews clarified that mediocrity would not be tolerated in this endeavour.

Dr Jaishankar had been consistent in his quest for excellence since his college days. We both studied at St. Stephen's College and JNU. When I joined JNU, I was fortunate to be on the same hostel floor as him. While that floor had its share of those just looking to get by, Dr Jaishankar stood out as a brilliant intellectual with a keen sense of the big picture, who never missed the woods for the trees. Even then, he inspired many of us, guiding us toward the civil services. I have always admired his razor-sharp intellect and clarity of thought. It was a pleasure to interact with him and seek his guidance during the year.

I also had the pleasure of working with Harsh Shringla, Chief Coordinator for the G20 presidency. He had vast experience as India's Foreign Secretary, as well as our Ambassador to key countries like the US, Bangladesh and Thailand. He's an extremely positive and constructive officer and it was wonderful collaborating with him in this massive endeavour.

Muktesh Pardeshi, OSD, G20 Operations, and L. Ramesh Babu, Joint Secretary, played focal roles in shaping the logistics for many meetings and ensuring seamless coordination. Rohit Ratish played a crucial role in the organization of the Leaders' Summit.

Sous-Sherpa Abhay Thakur, a seasoned diplomat, maintained a calm and level-headed demeanour that provided a steadying influence. His wealth of experience was invaluable, as he guided us through complex negotiations with a reassuring degree of skill. The balance he brought to our dynamic was instrumental in keeping discussions productive and focused on our common goals.

Joint Secretary (JS) Nagaraj Naidu, with his infectious exuberance and extensive UN experience and skills in geopolitical drafting, epitomized a can-do spirit that motivated us all. He had a knack for lightening the mood and even insisted on a quick yoga session during lengthy meetings to keep us focused and connected as a team.

Joint Secretary Eenam Gambhir brought remarkable energy to our G20 team. Her willingness to tackle challenging issues head-on and her passion for international diplomacy made her an invaluable asset. She approached every debate with zeal, advocating for the needs and interests of the Global South, and encouraging us to push boundaries.

Joint Secretary Ashish Sinha played an indispensable role in our journey. He brilliantly coordinated the third meeting of the G20 Sherpas in Hampi in July 2023, fostering collaboration on climate and energy issues, and negotiated closely with China.

Smriti, JS (Branding), brought both creative and practical insights into branding, successfully promoting India's image on the international stage with innovative initiatives that appealed to diverse audiences. Bhavna Saxena, JS (Security), coordinated closely with local law enforcement and international security teams to address potential threats, while implementing thorough protocols to protect delegates and facilitate smooth and safe operations at the various venues as high-level delegations from over 20 countries moved through 60 cities.

Additionally, the MEA deployed a team of dynamic young officers including Deepti Alanghat, Upasana Mohapatra, Akash Wankhade, Naman Upadhyay, and others, to the G20 Secretariat. They filled the Secretariat with lively energy, enhancing our preparations with new viewpoints.

I would particularly like to highlight the meticulous attention to detail of Anshuman Gaur, Chief of Protocol, for the Leaders' Summit. Coordinating the arrival and departure of the VIP aircraft, the traffic movement, and the presidential dinner for the leaders—these were mammoth undertakings involving extremely complex operational challenges, which he accomplished with great finesse.

As we prepared for the Summit, it became clear that the national capital simply didn't have enough space to accommodate the anticipated influx of VVIP jets. With over 100 aircraft, including a significant number of VIP jets, set to fly into the city, both the Indira Gandhi International (IGI) Airport and the Indian Air Force (IAF) base at Palam were falling short of space. Together they could handle only 40 aircraft, which presented us with a major logistical hurdle. The MEA had to quickly make alternative plans and decided to divert some flights to the nearby airports of Amritsar, Jaipur, Lucknow and Indore.

Adding to the complexity was the challenge of managing regular commercial air traffic. The commercial airlines were directed to cancel 20 to 25 per cent of their flights to make way for the VVIP arrivals, and Delhi International Airport Ltd (DIAL) received requests to cancel 80 domestic arrivals and as many departures during the three-day period.

We decided that IGI Airport would be the sole hub for all G20 flights to ensure that operations were centralized and manageable. Special arrangements were made to accommodate the VVIP aircraft, while 13 heads of state or delegates would arrive on commercial flights. In one particularly high-stakes meeting, the Chief of Protocol brought together officials from the Ministry of Home Affairs, the Indian Air Force, and the Bureau of Civil Aviation Security to discuss security measures and parking logistics. We realized early on that it was critical to keep runways open for incoming flights, but the parking demands were intensifying. The team brainstormed whether we could temporarily close one of the runways for parking, but DIAL representatives insisted that all runways were needed for landings during the summit. Amid these operational challenges, the constraint was reportedly exacerbated by 52 Airbus A320 aircraft from IndiGo and GoAir being grounded due to persistent engine issues, further complicating space availability.

To cope with the sheer volume of aircraft, we identified parking spaces at the IGI Airport for 40 Code 'E' jets for overnight stays and made provisions for an additional 70 aircraft on a rotational basis. We established four dedicated passenger terminals—known as Receptorium—ensuring they could seamlessly handle multiple VIP arrivals and departures simultaneously. Eventually, it became a well-oiled machine designed to handle the arrivals of leaders as quickly and smoothly as possible.

To further ease the influx of these high-profile guests, we created dedicated immigration and customs facilities at each terminal, offering expedited processing for all G20 delegations. Behind the scenes, a multi-agency coordination group worked tirelessly, providing unified flight clearances and addressing any emergent issues that arose, ensuring that our operations ran without a hitch.

Delhi Police played a pivotal role in the success of the G20 Summit in New Delhi, showcasing exceptional professionalism and dedication throughout the event. Their seamless adoption of advanced technology, coupled with meticulous traffic management, ensured that the complex logistics of such a large-scale international gathering were handled with precision. What truly stood out was their display of exemplary soft skills in human interaction, reflecting a level of sincerity and commitment that greatly contributed to the overall positive experience of the event.

Friends of Sherpa

Early on in my role as Sherpa, I quickly realized how important it was to create a space for myself where I could sift through the noise of endless discussions and express my ideas. While I was well-versed in governance and familiar with the complexities of the issues at hand, translating them into the nuanced language of diplomacy was a new challenge for me. It was clear to me that the subtleties of diplomatic dialogue required a different approach, one that balanced clarity with careful articulation. Realizing this, I sought a fresh set of eyes to join me—a group that had not yet grown weary of reading between the same lines. So, I formed a focus group comprising experienced retired foreign service officers that I aptly named 'Friends of Sherpa'. I engaged with the group virtually several times, to sound out ideas, gather insights, and refine our strategies for the G20 presidency, which proved instrumental through the course of the year-long process.

In our discussions within the group over video calls, Asoke Mukerji brought invaluable expertise from his extensive career, particularly from his role as India's Ambassador and Permanent Representative to the UN, where he oversaw negotiations on the 2030 Agenda for the SDGs. Asoke highlighted the significance of leveraging technology for effective implementation, reminding us to think strategically about what proposals would resonate and gain traction. His experience navigating complex intergovernmental negotiations helped us refine our approach, ensuring that we tackled pressing issues with a clear path to sustainable solutions.

On geopolitical relations, D. Bala Venkatesh Varma with his experience as India's ambassador to Russia, coupled with his knowledge of nuclear security, provided us with a carefully thought-out strategy for navigating sensitive issues. His input helped us to ensure that India's position remained both assertive and constructive amidst the backdrop of global tensions.

As the talks shifted to the pressing issue of climate change, Manjeev Singh Puri, who served as India's Ambassador to the EU and was a lead negotiator in various climate negotiations, brought a wealth of experience to our discussions on climate issues. His experience included pivotal roles in drafting agreements that shaped global climate policy, giving him a deep understanding of the intersectional complexities involved. The climate influences all aspects of life, making any discussion incomplete without considering its intersection with other areas of study.

Navigating the complexities of bilateral dynamics was also a challenge, and in these discussions, J.S. Mukul's extensive diplomatic experience became invaluable. As a former ambassador to the Netherlands, he advised on the nuances of diplomatic talks and emphasized the need for cultural sensitivity when it came to the interests of both developed and developing nations. His insights were invaluable in promoting cooperation rather than competition in our discussions.

Finally, Syed Akbaruddin, with his deep multilateral experience, offered critical counsel on engaging effectively with global stakeholders. His insights on leveraging social media for public diplomacy encouraged us to broaden our outreach and strengthen international ties. Drawing from his role as Chief

Coordinator of the third India-Africa Forum Summit in 2015, he provided valuable lessons on fostering cooperation among diverse nations.

This dynamic exchange turned my regular interactions with this group into a rich source of knowledge and inspiration. The relationships I built with these seasoned diplomats enriched my understanding and equipped me with the confidence and clarity to tackle the complex challenges of our G20 presidency.

Vinay Mohan Kwatra, then serving as Foreign Secretary of India, was an invaluable source of support to the G20 Secretariat during the summit in India. He deployed dynamic young officers to the G20 Secretariat and ensured that India's role as the host was executed with precision and professionalism. A seasoned diplomat with a wealth of experience in the IFS, he brought both strategic insight and operational effectiveness to the table.

Building a Legacy, Brick by Brick

As India prepared to host the G20 Leaders' Summit, the unveiling of the Bharat Mandapam in New Delhi in July 2023 by PM Modi was a defining moment for the nation, signalling not just an infrastructure upgrade but also a significant stride in the global MICE (meetings, incentives, conferences and exhibitions) sector. This sprawling facility, spread over 123 acres, symbolizes India's ambition to become a premier destination for international business events. Ranked among the world's top exhibition and convention complexes in terms of covered space available for events, Bharat Mandapam is a national endeavour that combines India's rich cultural heritage with state-of-the-art facilities.

What makes this venue particularly interesting is its unique architectural concept, which marries tradition and modernity. The shape of the building is inspired by the elegant form of the *shankha* (conch), which is a symbol of cultural pride often associated with purity and auspiciousness in Hindu rituals.

Apart from its cultural symbolism, the shankha shape provided practical advantages to the structure. Designed to optimize acoustics, it facilitates communication and engagement, making the venue ideal for large gatherings and conferences. Bharat Mandapam includes multiple meeting rooms, auditoriums and an amphitheatre, all equipped with advanced technology essential for hosting high-profile international events. The convention centre, adorned with paintings and tribal art forms from across India, depicts the fundamental elements of the universe—*akash* (sky), *vayu* (air), *agni* (fire), *jal* (water) and *prithvi* (earth), symbolizing India's holistic vision. This careful consideration of form and function highlights India's commitment to creating world-class infrastructure that meets modern demands.

The walls and facades intricately depict various facets of India's traditional art and culture such as *Surya Shakti*, which highlights solar energy initiatives, and the 'Zero to ISRO' exhibit, celebrating India's achievements in space exploration. These provided educational value and connected participants to India's advancements in various fields. They aimed to engage attendees in meaningful dialogue beyond the confines of business, fostering richer and more diverse conversations during their stay.

One of the crowning glories of the Bharat Mandapam is the 27-foot-tall bronze statue of Nataraja which is made of *Ashtadhatu* (an alloy of eight metals) and weighs about 18 tons. Crafted by renowned sculptor Radhakrishnan Sthapaty of Swami Malai in Tamil Nadu, this sculpture was completed in a record time of seven months, adding a spiritual and cultural dimension to the venue.

On 9 September, as the two-day G20 Leaders' Summit unfolded within its walls, the Bharat Mandapam emerged as a powerful symbol of India's aspirations and readiness to engage meaningfully with the global community. It was and continues to be a platform where critical discussions on global challenges can take place.

In tandem, the development of Yashobhoomi, conceived during my tenure as Chairman and CEO of Delhi Mumbai Industrial Corridor Development Corporation (DMICDC, now known as NICDIC), was accelerated solely by the G20 presidency. With a sprawling one million square metres of multipurpose space and the distinction of being India's largest convention and exhibition centre, Yashobhoomi represents a significant leap in India's ability to host large-scale events and positions the country as a global player in the MICE market.

Through their thoughtful design, state-of-the-art facilities, and cultural relevance, both Bharat Mandapam and Yashobhoomi establish India as a premier destination for national and international events, enhancing the country's stature on the world stage. As we move forward, this endeavour will undoubtedly create new opportunities for collaboration and innovation, boosting economic prospects and attracting the best of international business and political leadership.

An Inclusive Agenda

When the United Nations set out to formulate the SDGs a few decades ago, the hope was palpable. Nations rallied around a vision that aimed to eradicate poverty, promote sustainable economic growth, and ensure that no one was left behind. The goals reflected a collective aspiration—the belief that through global cooperation even the toughest challenges could be overcome. But over the years, the global order began to fragment. Divisions have deepened and the world feels increasingly cyclical, caught in a pattern where progress is followed by regression. The emergence of the Voice of the Global South serves as a call to action, demanding that the needs and perspectives of developing countries be recognized. This movement highlights the urgent need to create a more equitable global framework that recognizes our common future while addressing the disparities that divide us.

In January 2023, India kicked off its G20 presidency with the inaugural 'Voice of the Global South Summit'. The summit aimed to place the unique challenges faced by the Global South—especially the African continent—at the forefront of global discussions and reshape the dialogue to be inclusive and responsive to contemporary needs. This summit was PM Modi's bold declaration of intent. It conveyed to the world that the concerns and aspirations of nations of the Global South would take centre stage during India's tenure as G20 president. We aimed to bridge the gap between developed and developing nations, ensuring that the agenda focused on the pressing issues that truly mattered, such as development, trade and climate resilience.

The second pillar was the bold endeavour to secure a permanent seat for the African Union within the G20. This move recognized that Africa has a significant role in shaping global policies. Our goal was to democratize the G20, broadening its representation to create a more equitable platform. PM Modi's commitment to this cause was unwavering, and we aspired for discussions to culminate in concrete results that would redefine the G20's composition.

The third pillar focused on the aspirations of the countries of the Global South. While it remains important to address immediate needs, it is equally important to align G20 actions with the long-term vision for sustainable development. The current troika of India, Brazil and South Africa aptly represents the Global South on the international stage.

Lastly, we moved to transform the global approach to women's empowerment, advocating for initiatives that place women as leaders and partners in development. Our presidency was celebrated for negotiating impactful outcomes centred on gender equality and women-led development.

India's leadership during the G20 was significant for many reasons. It positioned the nation as a responsible and forward-thinking global player, committed to the greater good of humanity. The inclusive agenda showcased the importance of working together to tackle challenges such as climate change, economic disparities and gender inequality. By fostering an environment conducive to collaboration and dialogue, we built bridges between the Global North and Global South while reinforcing international partnerships. This spirit of collaboration created a constructive atmosphere within the G20, encouraging nations to put aside individual interests and work together for collective progress. India's commitment to an inclusive agenda during this presidency was a visionary step towards a more harmonious world.

During India's G20 presidency, substantial strides were made in reforming multilateralism. We amplified the voices of developing nations, championed development, and identified avenues for women-led initiatives. Reformed multilateralism emerged as a central theme, underscoring our commitment to giving the Global South a more prominent role in global decision-making.

As I reflect on this extraordinary year of the presidency, I feel that 'Vasudhaiva Kutumbakam' emerged as more than a mere slogan; it embodied a guiding principle for an inclusive and equitable future for humanity. Under PM Modi's leadership, India became a powerful advocate for the Global South, leaving an indelible mark on the global stage.

THREE

GREEN IT!

In the early 1800s, Henry Booth was mulling over how to solve the problem of engineering simple, long-distance communication between the world's first trains. Booth, an inventor and entrepreneur, probably had no idea how his innovations would ripple through time. By December 1868, the world's first traffic lights were installed in Parliament Square in London. This early railway signal used red to mean 'stop' and green to mean 'go', laying the foundation for centuries of global traffic systems.

It's fascinating how history spans time and connects us in strange, often unexpected ways. This colour-coded system designed to direct trains and traffic has transcended its original purpose, embedding itself into our collective consciousness. Red means stop, and green means proceed. These signals have not only guided our journeys on the roads but have also influenced our perception of progress and caution in different contexts.

I often thought about this while working on the draft for the New Delhi Leaders' Declaration (NDLD) for the G20 Summit. Just as those former engineers developed simple but profound systems to create order and progress, we set the stage for global cooperation and action. Our task was to draft a declaration that encapsulated the core messages we wanted to convey clearly and decisively—our own 'green light' for global initiatives.

There is a deeper psychological and cultural reason why red and green have prevailed as symbols. Red, associated with danger and urgency, naturally draws attention and signals the need to stop. This intense colour with the longest wavelength in the visible spectrum is highly visible and has been used throughout history for warning signals, from Roman war standards to alarms and emergency exits. It means humans are biologically hard-wired to recognize disaster from a distance. Yet in 2022, we found ourselves on the back foot, having lost decades of developmental progress to largely man-made catastrophes.

Meanwhile, green has always been home. We inherited a planet blessed with abundance, and it is our instinct to return to a natural state. Green evokes feelings of calmness, which makes it an ideal colour to signal a sense of security. These colour associations go beyond merely functional design. They resonate on a primal level, facilitating quick and instinctive responses.

Perhaps the phrase 'Green it' makes more sense in this linguistic continuum. These two words became a constant refrain of mine in the run-up to the New Delhi Leaders' Summit in September 2023. In the world of multilateral negotiations, a 'greened' text means consensus. All countries have agreed to the proposed language, and no further changes can be allowed. Given the paucity of time, my job was to colour as much text as green as possible. If I hadn't taken this approach, we would have run out of time and would not have reached a consensus.

In those final frenzied weeks, as we ploughed through the drafts and negotiated every clause, the phrase 'Green it' became our guiding mantra, steering us towards the finish line and a unified declaration from the G20 leaders.

Six Key Pillars, One New Approach

Our journey began on 4 December 2022 with the first meeting of all Sherpas amidst the serene surroundings of Lake Pichola in Udaipur. I gave a comprehensive presentation informing all the other Sherpas about India's ambitions and expectations for the year. I outlined India's priorities and the expected outcomes of the Sherpa Track. While each WG under the Sherpa Track had set its own priorities, I had clubbed various expected outcomes into overarching priorities.

Working closely with my team of young officers, we came up with six distinct pillars that represented the nation's priorities and its vision for global cooperation.

Strong, Sustainable, Balanced and Inclusive Growth

India set out with a bold vision for its G20 presidency, rooted in the endeavour to foster strong, sustainable, balanced and inclusive growth. With a burgeoning middle class projected to reach one billion people by 2046–47, we knew we needed to boost manufacturing and increase exports to achieve a remarkable annual growth rate of 9–10 per cent. PM Modi had long dreamt of an India of smart cities, where environmental sustainability and job opportunities are harmonized with a rapidly evolving technological landscape. To this end, we were committed to improving the ease of doing business both within and outside our borders by streamlining regulations and making significant investments in infrastructure to lay the groundwork for a vibrant, thriving economy.

Accelerating Progress on the SDGs

In the shadow of multiple global crises—pandemics, climate change and economic upheavals—India recognized the urgent need to push forward SDGs. We championed collective action, innovative financing solutions, and mobilization of private capital to breathe new life into global SDG efforts that had faced severe setbacks in recent years. At the meeting of development ministers in Varanasi in June 2023, India introduced and unanimously adopted the G20 Action Plan 2023 on Accelerating Progress on the SDGs. This document outlined key transformative areas like digital transformation, gender equality and sustainable transitions, fostering international partnerships and collaboration to meet these crucial goals.

Green Development Pact for a Sustainable Future

A profound respect for nature has been a cornerstone of India's approach to the environment, now finding a renewed expression through PM Modi's advocacy in the global climate discourse.

India's environmental consciousness, rooted in its ancient culture, has always advocated a symbiotic relationship with nature. The concept of *antyodaya*, which translates to uplifting the most vulnerable in society, has been ingeniously extended to climate action under India's leadership. This principle underscores the belief that genuine progress can only be achieved if it includes the welfare of the entire ecosystem, especially those most affected by environmental change.

India's call to action recognized that countries in the Global South are disproportionately affected by the impacts of climate change. The stress on fulfilling commitments under the United Nations Framework Convention on Climate Change (UNFCCC) and the Paris Agreement is as much a plea for adherence to international norms as it is a call for justice and equity in the global environmental order. It acknowledges that development and climate action must be two sides of the same coin, striking a balance between environmental protection and economic growth.

One of PM Modi's most significant contributions to the global environmental narrative is the concept of LiFE (Lifestyle for Environment). This initiative, launched by PM Modi at COP26 in Glasgow in November 2021, is a clarion call for collective and individual action, urging people worldwide to adopt a lifestyle that is in harmony with nature. LiFE was launched at the national level in Gujarat—a leader in renewable energy and climate initiatives. LiFE was already a significant and nationally valued concept. It reflects the ancient Indian practices where environmental protection and sustainability were ingrained in daily rituals and lifestyles. This traditional knowledge, passed down through generations, is now being championed by PM Modi on the global stage. By advocating for LiFE, he is not only highlighting India's rich environmental legacy but also providing a scalable and adaptable model for sustainable living worldwide, from conserving water and energy to reducing waste and embracing renewable resources.

LiFE posited everyone as a partner and stakeholder of the planet, advocating conscious use and not mindless consumption. Rather than adopting a top-down approach, LiFE promoted change from all angles—behavioural shifts, consumer choices, market incentives, and collective community action. It aimed to recognize and mobilize 'Pro Planet People', who practise a lifestyle harmonious with nature.

With LiFE, India sought to translate this vision into a measurable impact, mobilizing at least one billion global citizens to take individual and collective action for environmental conservation by 2028. Terminology was critical to India's leadership at the G20 as it was a key pillar of what was uniquely Indian and yet of global benefit. India's G20 presidency became a platform for amplifying this message of sustainable development and climate consciousness. India's emphasis on a nature-centred lifestyle is a testament to its commitment to lead by example in the fight against climate change. The G20 wholeheartedly welcomed and endorsed this vision under the High-Level Principles on Lifestyles for Sustainable Development.

Multilateral Institutions for the 21st Century

The global financial infrastructure needed an overhaul to meet the challenges of the 21st century. We pushed for the transformation of multilateral development banks like the World Bank and the IMF. Our efforts emphasized the urgency of incorporating climate action and cross-border issues in their mandates. Recognizing the limitations of government finances, we explored innovative strategies such as blended financing and sovereign green bonds. By tripling sustainable lending by 2030 and enhancing public-private collaboration, our vision was to build a resilient global economic system that fuelled sustainable growth.

Technological Transformation and Digital Public Infrastructure

Harnessing the power of technology was central to India's G20 agenda. India's remarkable achievements in digital public infrastructure (DPI) through initiatives like Digital India and the Aadhaar project have revolutionized public service delivery, ensuring transparency and efficiency. Through Pradhan Mantri Jan-Dhan Yojana (PMJDY), coupled with mobile technology and UPI, millions of people have been integrated into the formal banking system. By democratizing access to essential services, we enabled the digital inclusion of underserved communities and plugged leakages in Direct Benefit Transfers (DBTs) in India. The G20 was the perfect opportunity to showcase and streamline our models in global discourse. Our digital blueprint became a model for other nations, as we shared knowledge, best practices, and financial assistance to help low- and middle-income countries build their own inclusive, interoperable and secure DPI systems. By placing technology and digital infrastructure at the centre of our development agenda, our G20 presidency demonstrated how democratic values and inclusivity can drive global progress more holistically.

Gender Equality and Empowering All Women and Girls

Empowering women and girls was at the heart of India's G20 presidency. PM Modi laid the foundation of this initiative by emphasizing the importance of addressing issues like women's access to finance, entrepreneurship, and labour force participation. Initiatives such as *Beti Bachao Beti Padhao* emerged from these discussions, aiming to improve the sex ratio at birth and empower women from a young age. The Pradhan Mantri Ujjwala Yojana (PMUY) transformed rural kitchens by providing 96 million households with access to clean cooking fuel, specifically liquefied petroleum gas (LPG).[1] By switching from traditional biomass fuels, such as wood and coal, to cleaner alternatives, indoor smoke emissions were significantly reduced. As a result, women and children in rural households were able to breathe more easily, markedly reducing the number of respiratory diseases and preventable deaths.

The Swachh Bharat Mission (SBM) is one of India's biggest success stories. By 2019, the government of India had built over 100 million individual household toilets, declaring more than six lakh villages as open defecation-free (ODF), and aligned itself with SDG Target 6.2.[2]

Education and health initiatives such as Pradhan Mantri Matru Vandana Yojana (PMMVY), Mission POSHAN, and Pradhan Mantri Surakshit Matritva Abhiyan (PMSMA) ensured the well-being of women and children, addressing crucial aspects of their health. The government's efforts to destigmatize menstruation, a topic long shrouded in taboo, marked a significant cultural shift, which PM Modi himself addressed in his Independence Day speech. This change in narrative was reflected in the increasing use of safe menstrual products, as reported in the fifth National Family Health Survey (NFHS–5) 2019–21.

The financial empowerment of women was another cornerstone

---

[1]Pradhan Mantri Ujjwala Yojana 2.0, https://tinyurl.com/4643buk7. Accessed on 29 August 2024.

[2]World Health Organization, 'SDG Target 6.2 | Sanitation and hygiene: By 2030, achieve access to adequate and equitable sanitation and hygiene for all and end open defecation, paying special attention to the needs of women and girls and those in vulnerable situations', https://tinyurl.com/yck4csuj. Accessed on 29 August 2024.

of India's approach. Under the Pradhan Mantri Jan-Dhan Yojana, a massive financial inclusion initiative, women accounted for 56 per cent of the 50 crore bank accounts opened.[3] The surge in women-owned micro, small and medium enterprises (MSMEs) and the inclusion of female directors in start-ups underscored the growing role of women in India's economic landscape. Platforms like Mahila E-Haat and schemes such as MUDRA loans and the Sukanya Samridhhi Yojana have further bolstered women's financial independence and entrepreneurial spirit. Haat and schemes such as MUDRA loans and the Sukanya Samridhhi Yojana have further bolstered women's financial independence and entrepreneurial spirit.

The Women's Reservation Act 2023, although delayed, came at a crucial time, aligning with the physical, social and financial empowerment enabled by the government. With women constituting almost half of India's vast electorate, more women are now poised to enter public life and take on leadership roles, bringing essential perspectives to the political arena.

And so, India's G20 presidency, inspired by PM Modi's vision of an *Amritkaal* where *Nari Shakti* (the power of women) is celebrated, shifted the global focus from women's development to women-led development. This shift crystallized in the G20's NDLD 2023, which incorporated the Chair's Statement from the G20 Ministerial Conference for Women Empowerment. We were ambitious and aggressive about women-led development, moving away from the old UN terminology of gender equality. A lot of backroom negotiations had to be carried out to achieve this goal.

The Declaration's focus on strengthening economic and social empowerment, bridging the gender digital divide, promoting gender-inclusive climate action, and securing women's food security

---

[3]Ministry of Finance, 'Number of Jan Dhan Accounts Cross 50 Crore', https://tinyurl.com/2s35fyjz. Accessed on 29 August 2024.

and nutrition was a manifestation of India's commitment to gender parity. The establishment of a WG on women's empowerment, which convened during the subsequent Brazilian G20 presidency (2023–24), marked a significant milestone reflecting the collective commitment of G20 leaders to this cause.

I was happy to observe that India's priorities were welcome. But there were challenges too. Unlike other multilateral institutions, the G20 works by consensus, with no voting. My role was to ensure that all 20 members spoke with one voice. However, significant geopolitical tensions threatened to hinder progress. The issues of climate and energy transitions remained contentious between developed and developing nations, and the reform of multilateral institutions was another complex and divisive topic.

However, during this meeting, there was complete unanimity among all delegates when the opportunity arose to have the traditional *saafa* (turban) tied on their heads. This colourful experience quickly became a hit as the otherwise formally dressed delegates walked around the Manek Chowk, the palace ground of Udaipur's City Palace, with brightly coloured, sometimes oversized, turbans on their heads. Canadian Sous-Sherpa Gallit Dobner and EU Sous-Sherpa Martina Lodrant became the unexpected faces of the G20 social media as G20 platforms across India used their beaming smiles to capture the spirit of this gathering.

Interestingly, J.S. Nagaraj, who was also in charge of organizing this meeting, captured this photo. Amid all the fun, he snapped a few photos, not realizing that he would soon become a victim of his success. It turned out that he had a natural talent for photography, and soon, the communications team was hounding him for more pictures, clamouring for every shot he captured. What started as a casual click turned into a full-blown photography frenzy, leaving Nagaraj to juggle his duties and the burgeoning role of an unofficial G20 photographer.

If it was the saafa that turned heads at the first meeting, during the second Sherpa meeting in Kumarakom from 30 March to 2 April 2023 we made a statement by having all Sherpas don the traditional mundu, a garment deeply rooted in Kerala's culture.[4] As dignitaries from across the globe embraced this traditional wear, the atmosphere turned vibrant with a mix of cultures. However, getting everyone accustomed to the mundu proved to be quite a task. Many Sherpas wrestled with the complexities of keeping the garment from slipping. This led to some amusing moments as dignitaries were caught on camera mid-adjustment, leading to laughter and light-heartedness against the backdrop of the setting sun over the backwaters of Kerala. The local newspapers happily covered these softer moments, showcasing the more human side of the otherwise tough negotiations.

The delegates were also treated to the rich culture of Kerala: a traditional snake boat race, or the Chundan Vallam. As we looked out over Vembanad Lake, the longest lake in India, where four boats lined up, the sight of 128 oarsmen and their masters poised for action was both thrilling and symbolic. This regatta, usually held during the harvest season, was unique—two boats represented the G7, while the other two stood for the Emerging Markets, embodying the diverse perspectives we seek to balance within the G20.

The snake boat race is the ultimate example of coordinated teamwork, where each oarsman must synchronize their movements with precision to achieve victory. As the race began, everyone felt a collective surge of energy as we watched seemingly endless rows of oars slice through the water in perfect unison. The Emerging Markets won the first race, and in a spirited comeback, the G7 claimed the second race. The final race ended in a nail-biting

---

[4]The mundu, a long white or cream-coloured cloth wrapped around the waist, has been worn in South India for centuries, symbolizing local identity.

photo finish with no clear winner discernible. When the compere declared 'consensus has won', it was a light-hearted nod to our overarching goal of finding common ground amid our differing priorities and perspectives.

This race served as a powerful reminder of the collaborative spirit needed in our G20 discussions. We knew that we would soon return to the negotiation table, where the G7 would try to shift the focus to geopolitical issues like the Russia-Ukraine conflict, while the emerging economies pressed global challenges like poverty and climate change. This was a period of great upheaval, and great turbulence in the world, but ultimately the snake boat race reminded us of our ultimate goal—navigating complex waters together, proving that in the end the winner must be consensus.

It was towards this direction that I had internally directed my team, known as the Sherpa's Team in the G20 Secretariat, to start drafting a comprehensive and cohesive NDLD immediately after this meeting in Kumarakom. We decided to break away from the traditional method of structuring declarations by the WG, which often resulted in fragmented and disjointed documents. Previous declarations would isolate agriculture in one paragraph, culture in another, and so forth, failing to capture the interconnected nature of our challenges.

Instead, we took a cross-cutting approach. We identified six broad priorities, which became the key pillars of the NDLD. Each outcome from each WG was mapped to one of these six pillars. Within each pillar, we also established sub-pillars to ensure a detailed and multi-dimensional approach. This strategy enabled us to produce a document that was not only multidisciplinary but also aimed at directing solutions to the interlinked and compounding challenges of our time. My team worked tirelessly to integrate these elements, making the NDLD inclusive, ambitious, action-oriented and decisive, as mandated by PM Modi.

I was acutely aware of the need to avoid verbosity. In reviewing previous declarations with my team, it became clear that while there was plenty of text, there was often a lack of substance in terms of concrete actions and commitments from G20 countries. The language of the NDLD had to be leader-like, authoritative and clear, with explicit actions and commitments. To achieve this, we conducted a thorough review with all ministries leading the WGs. Each of the thirteen WGs under the Sherpa Track outlined their key deliverables. With this information, my team and I began drafting these outcomes in decisive and visionary language, steering clear of excessive technical details.

The preamble to the NDLD was particularly crucial, as it would be the most widely read element of the declaration. This section needed to clearly articulate the urgency of our challenges and the need for immediate action. Without a strong preamble, the NDLD would lack impact. We needed to achieve this in 600 words or less.

When I tell you that every word matters in the G20, I mean that quite literally. Comprehending diplomatic language required a crash course of its own. I learnt quite quickly that 'noting' was a polite and neutral way for countries to acknowledge the existence of a new policy without committing to it in any accountable way. 'Emphasizing' had more heft to it, while 'recall' or 'reaffirm' implied that an agreement had been reached in a previous discussion. For some countries, even 'recognizing' the fallout of war was against national policy and much of the negotiation was spent consolidating and distilling 20 opposing opinions into a single word. In the end, the aim is to agree and 'call upon' as much as possible so that the eventual declaration reflects actionable directives rather than a summary of views.

For anything to pass the impossible litmus test of such an exacting assimilation, compromise was necessary. And yet, as India's representative, I knew that 'noting' was not enough. Consensus could not come at the cost of the common person's interest. If India merely wanted a 'successful' presidency, measured solely by our ability to issue a joint Leaders' Declaration, we could have watered down our priorities. Pushing for a vast range of new initiatives was risky, especially in a deeply divided world that had so far paid more heed to political differences than collective responsibility.

At such a juncture in global dynamics, the world truly needed ambitious and decisive leadership, and PM Modi was determined to fill that vacuum. He believed it was our responsibility not only to uphold India's interests but also to advocate the needs of those who were marginalized by the changing tides of global politics. This unshakeable commitment made my role increasingly challenging as I grappled with the need for consensus while knowing that diluting our vision could lead to missed opportunities for real impact.

In retrospect, all those sleepless nights were worth it, although you'll have to ask my team separately what they feel about that! We celebrated the times we remained steadfast against the temptation to take the easy way out. Instead, we forged a declaration that aligned with our values and genuinely aimed to move the needle on pressing global issues. By prioritizing substance over superficial success, we ensured that our contributions would resonate beyond the immediate, making a real difference in the lives of people both in India and around the world.

Even as we were still shaping the G20 Leaders' Declaration, another significant responsibility rested on my shoulders. It was my job to integrate the paragraphs from the Finance Track into the final document. The traditional approach of the G20 is for the Finance Track to negotiate its language independently of the Sherpa Track, providing the text just before the Leaders'

Summit. While this practice had its merits, it often resulted in a declaration that felt disjointed, with noticeable differences in writing style and tone. We were determined to avoid presenting a fragmented document.

To ensure a cohesive declaration, we began to outline a cross-cutting document that included placeholders for the expected deliverables from the Finance Track. I communicated this strategy to Ajay Seth, Secretary, Department of Economic Affairs (DEA), who was the Finance Minister's deputy during India's presidency. I also shared what we referred to as the 'Minus One' and subsequent drafts with him. This collaboration aimed to create a more seamless final declaration, hoping to align the various sections for a consistent and unified tone.

Ajay Seth, with his forward-looking approach and commitment to collaboration, has been an invaluable partner throughout our work. He consistently brought a strategic, future-focused mindset to every challenge. I found his insights and dedication to be an incredible asset, enhancing the overall effectiveness of our team.

Beyond Structured Deliberations

On 30 June, we sent out the Zero Draft to all G20 countries and invitees, requesting written comments within a week. A few days later, I held a virtual meeting of all Sherpas during which I highlighted the key aspects, emphasizing our attempts to break from the past and create a lively, vibrant and cross-cutting document. Listening to the comments of the various Sherpas, I sensed that this could be the first time the G20 had seen such an effort. One comment comes to mind: the question of why digital skilling fell under the 'Future of Work' sub-pillar instead of the digital economy, considering it was to be covered by the Digital Economy Working Group. Similarly, digital health found its place under the 'digital ecosystems' in the technological transformation pillar. Again and again, I had to emphasize the cross-cutting nature of the document. We weren't merely listing outcomes by WG as we had in the past. This was different. We aimed to keep the declaration succinct and action-oriented, avoiding overly verbose additions.

We received written comments from G20 countries, each longer than the next. Rather than shortening the declaration, all countries stuck to the old tendency of adding blocks and blocks of long-winding text. With just a week to produce a new draft based on these comments, we dove head-first into a pool of endless bureaucratese with the utmost earnestness. The teams of Abhay, Nagaraj, Ashish and Eenam exhaustively reviewed all comments, cross-referencing suggestions with earlier declarations and signed agreements.

I worked closely with my team to complete what we were now calling the 'Rev 1' draft of the NDLD. We went through each comment, addition and deletion line by line with a fine-toothed comb. Some comments, for instance the inputs sent by the UK on the preamble, were extremely constructive. In other areas, we had to tread carefully, especially on issues close to developing countries, like climate finance. Balancing these inputs was crucial. I was fortunate to work with a team of experienced diplomats and subject-matter experts, which empowered us to fully defend the views of developing countries.

As we grappled with these challenges, some potential obstacles to reaching a consensus became apparent. It was a demanding process, but we pushed forward, fuelled by the conviction that this declaration would guide our common future.

By the third Sherpa meeting in Hampi, Karnataka, on 13 July, the first revised draft had gone out to all the Sherpas. Ashish Sinha led the organization of this crucial meeting. Not only were the logistics of the meeting seamless, but Ashish also ensured that delegates saw Hampi in all its splendour.

With the final summit just months away, the draft was still full of red lines. Tensions were high, with only the slightest wiggle room to navigate irreconcilable differences in geopolitics.

The G7 maintained that geopolitics couldn't be ignored, given the global ramifications of the war in Ukraine. However, several countries argued the G20 was not the forum for security discussions. Attempts to address this issue led to a stubborn impasse that dashed hopes of making progress on developmental priorities. We knew that if we delved into geopolitics in Hampi, a timely consensus for the New Delhi Leaders' Summit would remain a distant dream.

We deferred geopolitics for the fourth and final Sherpa meeting in New Delhi from 3 to 6 September, focusing instead on key developmental issues and striving for consensus in these areas. It took me some effort to convince everyone, but I was determined to stand my ground. The G20, as a body for international economic cooperation, needed to prioritize these issues.

We adopted an extremely transparent approach to the negotiations and ensured that no country felt that its voice was unheard. We made up a drafting team that recorded the G20 delegates' proposals in real time as we went around the room. The NDLD working draft was projected on multiple screens in the conference hall so that a multiple set of eyes accounted for every comma. Everyone could follow the positions of each country closely. We went line by line, paragraph by paragraph.

Clear points of difference emerged—especially around climate, energy transitions and multilateral reforms. In Hampi, we listened intently to each country's views, reflecting their feedback on the screen.

A few promising signs of progress emerged in the section on gender equality and women's empowerment. Our first draft was praised for its ambition, and Nagaraj played a seminal role in drafting and consolidating key parts of this text. However, challenges with the title of the section persisted. Terms like 'women-led development' and 'gender equality' met with resistance, with some countries preferring 'equality between men and women.'

By the time we left Hampi, it was clear that the progress I had hoped for remained elusive. With only one physical meeting of the Sherpas left, we were running out of time to tackle the biggest problem in the room—geopolitics.

July and August turned into a flurry of activity as WGs prepared for their Ministerial Meetings and my team and I engaged in several bilateral meetings. The finalization of Ministerial outcome documents provided us with the agreed-upon language to reference during negotiations. However, fraught discussions in several Sherpa Track WGs, like the Energy Transition Working Group, which failed to reach a consensus on key issues, signalled anticipated weak outcomes at the 28th Conference of the Parties (COP28) in the UAE later in the year.

In parallel to these larger discussions, ongoing bilateral meetings played a crucial role in winning hearts and minds behind the scenes while building personal relationships between representatives. These face-to-face, closed-door discussions, less marred by diplomatic talk and the limitations of formal negotiations, allowed the Sherpas to speak candidly and address each other's concerns openly. The importance of this personal rapport cannot be overstated—it was here that we truly understood the motivations driving each country, and were able to chart creative solutions and compromises that might not have surfaced in more structured and publicly scrutinized deliberations.

However, despite these efforts, we still hit a brick wall in August as numerous irreconcilable positions emerged. The stark differences in the priorities and perspectives of the delegations revealed the long road we still had ahead, a road we needed to traverse in record time.

Diplomacy 101

Counting solely on the final September meeting would jeopardize our success. We decided to hold daily virtual inter-sessional meetings throughout August. Starting at 2 p.m. Indian Standard Time, we would often work late into the night, pulling 8-, 10- and sometimes 12-hour workdays. Delegates from Brazil and Argentina logged in at 3 to 4 a.m. their time, while delegates from Australia joined at 9 p.m. Despite our packed agenda, I was acutely aware of the ticking clock.

Multilateral negotiations are inherently slow and iterative. Diplomats can spend hours, even days, discussing the same sentence. This was entirely new to me. As an administrator, I found this pace frustrating. We did not have the luxury of time, even if many were under the illusion that we did.

In the first virtual inter-sessional meeting, I launched into the discussions at breakneck speed. With the Development Ministers Meeting (DMM) already behind us, we could now move forward with its key outcomes: the G20 2023 Action Plan on Accelerating SDGs and the High-Level Principles on LiFE. Initially, we had slated a week for these negotiations. Given that a consensus was reached at the DMM just a couple of weeks ago, I assumed we would be able to breeze through these issues.

However, when a flood of long-winded comments started pouring in from various countries—packed with repetitive text, unnecessary context, or attempts to alter the meaning—I had to stand my ground. I resolutely navigated through each draft, ensuring the process remained streamlined and efficient.

After each paragraph, I would collate all country views and dictate the revised text live, maintaining complete transparency. Then I would reopen the floor for comments but this time only pertinent suggestions were entertained. 'Green it,' I would instruct my drafting team when we had reached a consensus, signalling that the text was final and unchangeable. This phrase became my mantra throughout the inter-sessional meetings. The G20 negotiators were unprepared for the pace at which we progressed, wrapping up the entire week's agenda in just one day. Many had expected our sessions to drag on as usual but by the end of the first day, significant parts of the NDLD were 'greened'.

This break from past practices was invigorating, but I knew I should not celebrate prematurely. Diplomatic negotiations often involve 'bracketing' text—placing contentious phrases or sentences in square brackets, indicating they are still open for discussion. When we encountered particularly thorny issues, I instructed my team to put them in brackets and move on, greening the remaining text. Time was of the essence, and we would return to those bracketed items later. Many contentious issues required this careful back and forth, but with each step we moved closer to a consensus.

Nevertheless, we faced major challenges. China opposed all issues where India-led terminology was used. Vasudhaiva Kutumbakam, LiFE, and women-led development were tactically opposed. In the Development Working Group (DWG), consensus could only be reached if we used the term 'Lifestyles for Sustainable Development' (as opposed to environment). We tried various permutations: LiFE in brackets after Lifestyles for Sustainable Development, or even LiFEstyles for Sustainable Development. Each time, we faced opposition—not because of the content, which had been greened earlier, but simply because of the terminology.

Building a personal rapport became our strategy to overcome these hurdles. In a series of bilateral meetings at the Sherpa level, my team and I had candid discussions with the Chinese delegation. We expressed our desire to collaborate and pointed out that their tactical opposition was counterproductive. We also listened patiently to their views. These open dialogues helped build bridges, which eventually led to a consensus that paid off richly in the long run. I must credit Abhay Thakur and Ashish Sinha for their ceaseless efforts in these negotiations.

Despite these efforts, the pace of negotiations crawled to a halt in the days that followed. The countries pulled every excuse to avoid completing text. 'We'll have to check with our experts' became the refrain. 'This wasn't scheduled for today,' was another favourite. 'We'll run it through our system,' they'd say, stalling us further. It was clear these were delaying tactics meant to drag out the proceedings.

Internally, our strategy was firm: avoid getting backed into a corner where we'd have to concede on key priorities just to get the joint declaration out the door. Occasionally, there were genuine cases where the negotiators needed to consult with their line ministries or experts. However, I knew these experts would likely return with lengthy, convoluted sentences that were of little real use.

With a pinch of humour, I encouraged the negotiators to bypass their line ministries, as their approach would be very technical and not consensus-oriented. But I also understood the importance of managing energy levels, especially for those joining at odd hours. Part of my strategy was to let the delegates wear themselves out. Once fatigue set in, I'd seize the moment to push through rounds of 'greening' the text. There was always some resistance, but in these moments of fatigue, I could often tip the scales in our favour.

However, there were several red lines or sensitivities that we had to navigate in our quest for consensus. In the preamble, Saudi Arabia was adamantly opposed to linking the term 'crisis' with 'climate change', insisting on 'challenge' instead. It is important to remember that the economies of many countries continue to depend heavily on oil, and such terms could have far-reaching implications for their economic policies and global standing. This is diplomacy 101: balancing the nuanced interests and sensitivities of various nations to find common ground. This sparked more friction in the room, leading to intense discussions. Finally we reached a compromise, incorporating both terms in paragraph 3 of the preamble: 'Years of cascading challenges and crises have reversed gains in the 2030 Agenda and its Sustainable Development Goals (SDGs).'[5]

In the same paragraph, another sentence became another bone of contention. Rising energy inflation has massively increased the cost of living across the world. Some countries objected to the exclusive use of the term 'energy prices', insisting that the high inflation was a consequence of rising energy 'commodity prices', and not just energy prices alone.

One of the most exhausting tasks was dealing with the verbosity of written and oral comments. Multilateral documents are often a chore to read, filled with convoluted language that obscures their true meaning. I often urged delegates to cut the fluff. Phrases like 'Don't teach us English' and 'Don't add unnecessary text' became part of my daily conversations. Despite my best efforts, these pleas often fell on deaf ears. Some delegates were determined to dictate long-winded sentences that contributed little to the substance of the document. On several occasions, I had to firmly reject these suggestions, urging them to be constructive and concise.

---

[5]'G20 New Delhi Leaders' Declaration', New Delhi, India, 9–10 September 2023, https://tinyurl.com/t6dzsa69. Accessed on 6 September 2024.

I felt that many developed countries were using cleverly disguised language to shirk their responsibilities. Our proficiency in the English language allowed us to swiftly identify such attempts to camouflage responsibilities through subtle language tweaks. For example, a sentence in the NDLD discussing the financial needs for climate action originally read: 'Note the need of USD 5.8–5.9 trillion in the pre-2030 period required for developing countries, in particular for their needs to implement their NDCs, as well as the need of USD 4 trillion per year for clean energy technologies by 2030 to reach net zero emissions by 2050.' Some English-speaking countries suggested changing 'required for' to 'required in', which would completely shift the burden of funding onto developing countries. We argued that the funds should be channelled to developing countries. The proposed alternative would put the onus on developing countries to raise funds for climate action, rather than developed ones. We stood firm, ensuring the phrase 'for developing countries' was retained. As countries played semantic games, we were able to effectively counter and keep the focus where it belonged.

To keep the document action-oriented, I was forced to shut down their interventions. Judging by the reactions of the seasoned diplomats in my team, I realized this was not very diplomatic of me, but my goal was clear—we wanted consensus, and we wanted a document that went beyond mere rhetoric.

On the third or fourth day, the delegates began to apologize before suggesting a new text. I insisted that if they were going to add text, they should also be prepared to cut elsewhere. Of course, countries tended to delete text unfavourable to them, and so the task fell to my team and me for trimming the unnecessary filler words.

Our Zero Draft started with around 6,000 words but ballooned to over 9,500 after incorporating comments from the countries.

After working day and night, we managed to trim it to around 6,500 words, retaining all the country inputs while staying true to our core message. This was no small feat—it's often harder to write less than more. It requires clarity of thought, vision, and a deep understanding of the issues at hand.

There were days when progress was excruciatingly slow. I remember one particularly gruelling session where delegates spent close to seven hours working on a single paragraph on climate action. We ended up drafting and redrafting that paragraph at least twenty times, and in the end, we could only manage to put it in brackets. The divide between the developed countries and the developing ones became increasingly visible, with each side entrenched in its position.

I remember that the last paragraphs became contentious when the discussion turned to who would host the G20 after South Africa's presidency in 2025. As every G20 country had held the presidency at least once, the cycle was to start afresh. But here too, bilateral issues threatened to overshadow the entire process. The proposal that the US should preside over the G20 in 2026 met with stiff resistance. The trade tensions between the US and China, coupled with geopolitical strains with Russia, resulted in a lengthy debate. As Chair, I had to play an impartial role as an honest broker.

I knew in part that the US was seeking a presidency to break the supremacy of the Global South in the Indonesia-India-Brazil-South Africa quartet. Internally, the US was also grappling with tumultuous domestic politics that had undermined its decades of global influence. Internationally, there was growing concern about China's accelerating rise. The scales were tipping, and the US saw India as a vital buffer to counterbalance China's ascendance. But India was so much more than that. Our leadership in the Global South and our stated position as a reformer of multilateral institutions made us a threat to the status quo. India was an ally of many, forging partnerships based on mutual respect and common goals, but we were not a pushover. The current global order would not last, and everyone in the room was acutely aware of this fact.

Touch of Humour

Not all negotiations were devoid of lighter moments. For instance, France wanted to include a mention of the 2024 Olympic Games in the NDLD. Naturally, this raised eyebrows. Delegates questioned why we should single out the Olympics when other significant global sporting events were on the horizon. In jest, I suggested we include the 2023 Cricket World Cup and the 2024 T20 World Cup as well.

And then, amid heated negotiations on climate action, India made history on 23 August 2023 with the Chandrayaan mission, becoming the first country to land on the lunar south pole. We took a moment to break the tension and streamed the landing live for everyone. The room buzzed with excitement and appreciation, and Russia even suggested acknowledging India's achievement in the final NDLD. Moments like these reminded us of our shared experience of humanity on this planet and the potential for unity despite our differences.

Another instance was the informal 'exam' for internal consultants held at the Sushma Swaraj Bhawan, where they were quizzed on all past G20 declarations and commitments. Nagaraj, with his trademark enthusiasm, even took on the role of the invigilator. He paced the room, pretending to be the strictest supervisor on the planet. The consultants murmured, 'Is he really going to check our papers like we're back at school?' With a playful grin, Nagaraj leaned over a desk and said, 'I hope you're not trying to peek at your neighbour's answers! Save the collaborating for the negotiating table.' He then resumed walking, his laughter bouncing off the auditorium walls. With each exaggerated peek over his shoulder and theatrically raised eyebrow, Nagaraj turned what could have been a stressful day into an extraordinary exercise in both teamwork and light-heartedness. By the time the 'exam' ended, the room was full of smiles.

It reminded everyone that even while working day and night on weighty issues, a touch of camaraderie and humour went a long way, particularly in the days leading up to the Leaders' Summit.

FOUR

ON THE PATH TO GREEN DEVELOPMENT

The negotiations surrounding the climate paragraphs at the G20 meetings were undoubtedly among the toughest, rivalling those on geopolitics in terms of complexity and controversy. This arduous process can be attributed to rising concerns over energy and growing socio-economic pressures, such as the ongoing cost-of-living crises. Geopolitical tensions have further heightened uncertainties regarding a stable supply of fossil fuels, a situation exacerbated by the Ukraine-Russia conflict. These developments have exposed the vulnerabilities in our energy systems and underscored the stark reality that over-reliance on fossil fuels jeopardizes both economic stability and environmental sustainability.

Fossil fuels remain a contentious issue because of their dual impact on the economy and the environment. Their significant contribution to greenhouse gas emissions has escalated climate change, causing severe environmental damage. However, transitioning away from these sources of energy poses substantial challenges, particularly for economies heavily reliant on fossil fuel revenues. Policymakers are under pressure from powerful fossil fuel lobbies, resulting in slow progress in implementing meaningful climate policies.

The discourse has often been dominated by vague language that sidesteps addressing the root causes of climate change. The emphasis on energy security—especially considering recent geopolitical tensions—has further stymied serious discussions about transitioning away from fossil fuels.

This has brought the deeply entangled relationship between economic realities and climate commitments to the forefront, creating a complicated landscape for international cooperation, particularly within democratic forums like the G20. Together, G20 nations account for approximately 75 to 80 per cent of the world's total greenhouse gas emissions.[1] Energy security has long influenced the discourse on climate commitment, leaving the G20 nations at a crossroads where they must reconcile economic imperatives with climate obligations. Balancing the urgent need for energy security with the pressing demand to mitigate and adapt to climate change has created a web of interests, opinions and trade-offs.

However, the world sees the G20 as a positive next step, primarily because of its role as a unique forum for major economies. This diverse group encompasses a mix of developed, developing and emerging economies, reflecting a recognition that all nations must share the responsibility for climate action and the transition, considering historical emissions.

Therefore, when G20 nations come together to discuss commitments, they are sending a powerful message to the global community that the world's major economic powers—which largely drive greenhouse gas emissions—are ready to engage in constructive dialogue and cooperation to tackle the shared challenges of balancing socio-economic and climate goals. This forum is a pivotal step forward as it plays a significant role in shaping international climate commitments, particularly in the run-up to the COP meetings. Discussions within the G20 foster common ground, encourage collaboration, and identify areas of convergence, setting the stage for more ambitious and comprehensive agreements at the COP. Essentially, the G20 serves as a litmus test for the willingness of major economies to commit to meaningful climate action. The G20 has the potential to show that economic prosperity and climate responsibility can coexist, offering hope amidst the urgent challenges facing the world.

---

[1] D'souza, Renita, and Debosmita Sarkar, 'Climate Performance Index: A Study of the Performance of G20 Countries in Mitigation', *Observer Research Foundation*, 20 February 2023, https://tinyurl.com/4uh33jef. Accessed on 7 September 2024.

I firmly believe that the G20 should consider tackling climate change, sustainable development and economic growth holistically, recognizing the inherent interconnectedness that binds these critical issues. Climate change, with its adverse environmental impacts, poses a substantial threat to the SDGs and economic stability. Failing to address this challenge risks unravelling the very fabric of economic progress and prosperity.

Balancing Climate and Development: A Delicate Equilibrium

India's G20 presidency delivered a powerful message for the coming decade: climate change and economic development are two sides of the same coin and must be central to the G20 agenda. In a world where the balance between growth and environmental stewardship is increasingly being scrutinized, India has consistently underscored that tackling climate change is not merely an option but an imperative—this belief is underpinned by our domestic achievements and initiatives. India has championed this pragmatic approach while recognizing the unique vulnerabilities of the Global South.

The historical emissions data tell a compelling story: developed nations, particularly in the Global North, have contributed the overwhelming majority of carbon emissions, a legacy of what can only be described as 'atmospheric colonization'. For example, from 1850 to the end of the last decade, developed countries accounted for a staggering 79 per cent of historical carbon emissions.[2] Further, they are also responsible for more than 90 per cent of excess global carbon emissions, often relying

[2]'Developed Countries Are Responsible for 79 Percent of Historical Carbon Emissions', Center for Global Development, https://tinyurl.com/bdh56cxs. Accessed on 7 September 2024.

on resources and labour sourced from the developing world which bears the brunt.[3]

Given the ambitious pledges made by more than 190 countries under the Paris Agreement to limit global temperature rise to well below 2°C, the Global South faces daunting challenges in navigating a scarce carbon space. It's astonishing to realize that developed nations have consumed more than 80 per cent of the global carbon budget, leaving barely enough room for developing nations to support their development aspirations. As someone who has spent a large part of his career by the coast in Kerala and has been shaped by the ecologies that inform a symbiotic relationship between humans and nature, I believe that addressing climate change must be rooted in principles of fairness and equity. Developed countries must take the lead in cutting their domestic emissions while supporting developing countries on their path to sustainable development through cost financing and technology transfer.

Article 9 of the Paris Agreement stipulates this responsibility, clearly stating that developed countries are obligated to provide financial resources to assist developing countries in their climate efforts. To this end, developed countries have committed to a common goal of mobilizing $100 billion annually by 2020 for climate action in developing countries, but have consistently failed to meet this target. Australia, Canada and the US, for example, are lagging well behind in fulfilling their international climate finance commitments. It's particularly disheartening to note that the US, despite having an economy 40 per cent larger than the EU, has managed to mobilize just five per cent of its fair share of

---

[3]Hickel, Jason, 'Quantifying national responsibility for climate breakdown: an equality-based attribution approach for carbon dioxide emissions in excess of the planetary boundary', *The Lancet* Planetary Health, September 2020, Volume 4, Issue 9, E399-E404, https://tinyurl.com/636nd525. Accessed on 7 September 2024.

climate finance in 2020, just one-twelfth of what it should have provided. Australia and Canada also fell short with contributions of only 23 per cent and 18 per cent of their fair share, respectively, and neither showed a clear commitment to a meaningful increase by 2025. This ongoing neglect further exacerbates the plight of developing countries that desperately need financial support to which they are rightfully entitled.[4] It's particularly disheartening to note that the US, despite having an economy 40 per cent larger than that of the EU, has managed to mobilize just 5 per cent of its fair share of climate finance in 2020, just one-twelfth of what it should have provided. Australia and Canada also fell short with contributions of only 23 per cent and 18 per cent of their fair share, and neither showed a clear commitment to a meaningful increase by 2025. This ongoing neglect further exacerbates the plight of developing countries that desperately need the financial support they are rightfully entitled to.

Compounding the inadequacy of climate finance, the Global South now grapples with a series of cascading crises. The pandemic, the skyrocketing cost of living, and rising interest rates have pushed many developing nations to a critical juncture where they face an impossible choice: implementing tough economic measures or sacrificing investments needed to achieve the SDGs. The devastating impacts of climate change on progress on the SDGs through interconnected crises call for a unified approach—one that recognizes the intricate web of dependencies linking these challenges. The path forward demands not just acknowledgement but decisive action that interlaces climate responsibility with developmental ambitions.

I have witnessed the precariousness of this situation firsthand.

[4]OECD, *Climate Finance Provided and Mobilised by Developed Countries in 2013-2021*, 16 November 2023, https://tinyurl.com/9s889kff. Accessed on 7 September 2024.

The countries in the Global South are caught in a dual battle against climate change and the urgent need to realize the SDGs. Halfway to the deadline for the 2030 Agenda for Sustainable Development, it became painfully clear that we were leaving more than half of the world behind. Many countries are reversing more than 30 per cent of their SDGs. Investments to meet these goals had stalled, with developing nations facing an annual funding gap of $4 trillion—an increase from $2.5 trillion in 2015 when the SDGs were first adopted.[5] This funding shortfall has led to unsustainable debt levels, making these countries vulnerable to economic shocks, similar to the 1980s debt crisis that crippled many developing borrowers. Currently, around 60 per cent of low-income countries are either in a state of debt distress or at significant risk, a figure that has nearly doubled since 2015. Repayments now consume 11.3 per cent of government revenue in these countries, up from 5.1 per cent in 2010, highlighting the urgent need for a reformed international financial architecture.

This architecture, established years ago, is woefully inadequate to meet today's challenges. The frameworks, policies and operations of these institutions are no longer compatible with the needs of the current global landscape, particularly in the Global South. There is an interesting necessity to overhaul the international financial institutions (IFIs) and the multilateral development banks to make them more inclusive, flexible, and attuned to the unique requirements of developing countries.

The countries of the Global South face a myriad of financial constraints in climate investments. Foreign exchange exacerbates the high cost of borrowing in foreign currencies, a significant obstacle that risks creating volatility and affects financial decision-making. The lack of blended finance mechanisms, which integrate

---

[5]UN Trade and Development (UNCTAD) 2023, *World Investment Report 2023*, https://tinyurl.com/fuus5cpp. Accessed on 7 September 2024.

public and private funds, compounds this scarcity of financial resources for climate initiatives. Inadequate project development capacities and the lack of national project pipelines further limit the ability of these countries to effectively plan, implement and monitor strategic climate projects. These complicated financial dynamics, coupled with a not-fit-for-purpose international financial architecture, require an unprecedented approach to solving these intertwined challenges.

In my discussions with PM Modi, the urgency of pressing ahead with climate action became increasingly clear. After all, he had maintained unequivocally, 'For me, this is a moral issue. You don't have a right to exploit what belongs to future generations. We are only allowed to milk the earth, not to kill it.'[6]

However, it was clear that any approach must resonate with the development priorities of the Global South. Together, we recognized the need for a more inclusive framework to unify emerging markets on this pressing issue. This led to the introduction of the term 'Green Development'—a concept that encapsulates climate action, sustainable development, energy transition, a circular economy, and ocean health. By embracing the interconnectedness of these challenges, we can coordinate global efforts that not only protect our planet but also stimulate economic growth for all nations, particularly those in the Global South. India's presidency endeavoured to take the successes at home and the lessons learnt from the Voice of the Global South Summit to the G20 stage, securing consensus on the much-needed 'Green Development Pact for a Sustainable Future' alongside the Action Plan for SDGs.

However, the path to consensus was anything but straightforward. With the summit drawing near and the stakes higher than ever,

[6]Antholis, William J., 'India's Climate Change Policy in a Modi Government', *Brookings*, 30 July 2014, https://tinyurl.com/mtbbnrvw. Accessed on 10 September 2024.

the stage was set for one of the most challenging negotiations yet. What unfolded next would define not only the direction of the G20 but also India's role in shaping a sustainable future.

Playing Jenga at Different Levels

When comparing energy and climate negotiations, it is essential to recognize that these are two distinct issues, although they are closely linked. Climate negotiations are bound by legal barriers such as the UNFCCC positions, the Paris Agreement Commitments, and the principles of common but differentiated responsibilities and respective capabilities that impose strict guidelines and limitations. In contrast, there is no such legal baggage in energy transition discussions, giving us the freedom to explore options and make unprecedented decisions, unencumbered by pre-existing constraints.

Consider the game of Jenga, where players begin with a tower of wooden blocks. Each player removes a block from the structure and places it on top, making the tower more unstable with each move. Climate negotiations are similar to a Jenga at level 28, where the tower is already precariously balanced, and each move is fraught with the risk of collapse. Numerous agreements create a rigid framework, limiting the flexibility of negotiations.

On the other hand, energy transition discussions are like playing Jenga at level 4. The structure is still stable, providing more room for innovative solutions and creative problem-solving, unbound by the same level of legal constraints.

In the overall text of the NDLD, the Green Development section is the largest. It makes up 28 per cent of the total text. Four Sherpa Track WGs—Energy Transitions (ETWG), Environment and Climate Sustainability (ECSWG), Development, and Disaster Risk Reduction (constituted by India in 2023)—have played pivotal roles in contributing to this section. These WGs feed into the final NDLD, with Sherpas from all G20 countries negotiating and agreeing to include the most critical outcomes. While many critical outcomes of the Development and Disaster Risk Reduction WGs were agreed upon unanimously early on, the ETWG and ECSWG presented significant challenges.

Amidst these challenges, bridging the gap between historical responsibilities, current geopolitical realities, and the urgent need for collective action became an intimidating task for me as Chair. This required a mix of technical solutions and delicate diplomacy that I hoped would foster trust and confidence among nations with competing interests.

To this end, I was in constant contact with my team deployed at the energy transition and climate meetings, where they tirelessly negotiated day and night. We discussed the issues that were either resolved or close to consensus, ensuring we were ready for the Sherpa-level meetings.

In the climate working group, some crucial outcomes remained contentious and were listed in the Chair's Summary as non-consensus text. This deadlock included issues like reaching the global emissions peak by 2025 and an absolute emissions reduction target by 2030/2035. These challenging points were later negotiated extensively, and an agreement was reached at the Sherpa level.

A similar scenario unfolded in the energy transition group, where seven out of 29 paragraphs were deadlocked and incorporated only as a Chair's Summary, impeding key outcomes such as tripling the global renewable energy capacity, phasing out fossil fuels, and establishing open, competitive, non-discriminatory and free international energy markets. These were also hammered out later during Sherpa-level negotiations and included in the final declaration.

The inclusion of these outcomes from the Chair's Summary in the Leaders' Declaration was pivotal—it sent a strong, balanced signal to the upcoming COP28 discussions, emphasizing a united front on crucial climate and energy issues.

Hundreds of hours of negotiations must have gone into the discussions on hydrogen, and bafflingly, much of this time was spent debating its colour. While the countries agreed in principle that hydrogen is an alternative fuel for the future, each country brought its colour to the table. India staunchly advocated for green hydrogen, which uses renewable energy for the electrolysis process to separate hydrogen and oxygen from water. Meanwhile, other countries proposed blue hydrogen, grey hydrogen, and even turquoise hydrogen. These colour-coded debates seemed never-ending, with the conversation veering towards options that included fossil fuel-powered hydrogen—a prospect that would defeat the purpose.

Unable to reach consensus at the working group level, the contentious issue of green hydrogen was escalated to the Sherpa Track. Even then, it met resistance. Some countries argued that if the working group could not reach an agreement, then the issue shouldn't be discussed at the Sherpa level either. In the end, however, we finally did clinch green hydrogen at the Sherpa level.

Recognizing that the energy and climate negotiations would require intense discussions, we logged over 400 hours of virtual negotiations before the fourth Sherpa meeting in Delhi in September 2023, meticulously addressing non-contentious texts. We reached a consensus on issues like the circular economy, LiFE, ecosystem restoration, ocean-based economy, ending plastic pollution, and disaster risk resilience. However, fossil fuels, carbon capture and utilization, climate finance, and technology transfer proved far more elusive.

The fourth Sherpa meeting saw over 150 hours of gruelling negotiations on climate and energy, supplemented by many bilateral meetings. Saudi Arabia remained firm on fossil fuels and the circular carbon economy, strongly resisting any talk about phasing down or phasing out fossil fuels. The country's Sherpa, Abdulmuhsen Alkhalaf, was not an official diplomat but proved to be a tough negotiator on climate and energy issues. He supported the emerging markets and was clear about the need for our success. Without Saudi's agreement, the entire negotiated text was in danger of collapsing like a house of cards. My team and I spent days in tense negotiations with the Saudi delegation. At one critical stage, I had to call upon Dr Jaishankar to address his Saudi counterpart to break the deadlock.

To make matters worse, China's astute negotiating team often leveraged multilateral foray to push bilateral issues. During the energy transition negotiations, the Chinese delegation even brought up language about semiconductor technologies—a completely unrelated issue but a major point of contention with the US. I had to request both delegations to handle this issue bilaterally to ensure that we could move forward with the consensus of all parties.

As the tension in the meeting room reached its peak, we knew that the outcome of our efforts would be either a breakthrough or a deadlock. The stakes had never been higher, and the last hours of negotiations would define not just the success of the summit, but also the future trajectory of global climate and energy policies.

The Sherpas understood the pressure we were under. Most of the countries at the table had held the presidency before and knew exactly what it took to organize such a significant event. However, as an emerging economy and a representative voice of the Global South, the pressure on India was even greater. We could not afford to let down a bloc of nations eager to change their destiny through our leadership. In moments of high tension like these, a well-timed joke acted as a lifeboat, guiding us back to friendly territory. The Sherpas often exchanged quips, and I couldn't help but wonder if their humour in part bolstered my spirits during our discussions. This unspoken kinship carried me through my toughest moments. Although we were on opposing sides of many arguments, we were also each other's direct counterparts. Next year, the roles would be reversed with a different nation at the helm, but the kindness and support would carry over.

As we were getting by with little more than coffee and commitment, one of us jokingly suggested that a boxing match should resolve the key issues of energy and the environment outside the venue. The laughter that erupted punctured the tense atmosphere and allowed us to breathe a little easier. At that moment, the humour not only provided a welcome distraction but also reminded us that amidst the weight of our responsibilities, we could still find joy and solidarity in our common mission.

Coffee, Commitment, and Consensus

During the negotiations, the key was to understand the unique challenges faced by developing and emerging economies—particularly their need for substantial carbon space to fuel socio-economic growth. However, countries heavily dependent on fossil fuels demanded equivalent ambition for other zero- and low-emission technologies, including carbon abatement and removal technologies. We tirelessly advocated for a balanced and equitable resolution.

The turning point came when India, along with other emerging markets, pushed for an approach that transcended the traditional Global North-South divide. We meticulously highlighted the financial need for developing countries in the pre-2030 period, articulating the need for $5.8 to $5.9 trillion to support the transition towards implementing their nationally determined contributions. This underscored the financial burden on developing economies by highlighting the interconnectedness of global climate goals within diverging economic realities.

This innovative approach bridged the gap between developing and developed nations, allowing both sides to find common ground. Developed nations pledged the monumental financial support required for this transformative journey and together we committed to the ambitious emissions reduction targets. In this tale of diplomatic finesse, India emerged as a catalyst for unity, crafting an outcome that transcended traditional divisions and propelled the world toward a more sustainable future.

But the story doesn't end here.

The triumph over financial commitments for developing countries soon faced an unexpected hurdle. Some developed countries, steadfast in their reservations, called for a closer examination of the geopolitical paragraphs before fully backing the outcome, which emphasized the urgent need for $5.8 to $5.9 trillion of investment before 2030 for effective climate action. In a surprising twist, the destiny of one of the key climate outcomes teetered on the brink of being 'hijacked' by geopolitical complexities—an unprecedented development in the G20 landscape.

The turning point came through the solid diplomatic relations PM Modi had cultivated with the heads of state of the G20 member countries. Through deft negotiations and the strategic use of these connections, we navigated the geopolitical labyrinth, ultimately ensuring the integrity of our balanced climate agenda. In a striking demonstration of the power of strategic diplomacy, we not only preserved this historic climate outcome but also averted a crisis that could have unravelled the delicate equilibrium achieved during the G20 negotiations.

Ultimately, India's presidency achieved what was considered almost impossible: securing an ambitious and groundbreaking outcome on energy at the G20. We reached a consensus on the ambitious 'Green Development Pact for a Sustainable Future'. The outcomes encapsulated in this pact—tripling global renewable energy capacity by 2030, calling for trillions in climate finance, and setting a daunting 43 per cent emissions reduction target—stand as cornerstones for the final agreement at COP28. The landmark agreement to triple global renewable energy capacity by 2030 and double energy efficiency, pivotal for reducing global clean energy costs and meeting the Paris Agreement commitments, required a massive undertaking in just seven years. Developing countries, including India, played a crucial role in shaping the final language.

By aligning climate commitments with the developmental ambitions of the Global South countries, India has positioned itself as a true Voice of the Global South. At the G20 table, we advocated a harmonized approach to climate action, amplifying the voices of developing nations and striving for seamless integration of climate goals with developmental objectives.

Reflecting on this experience, my role as a G20 Sherpa was anchored in a deep-seated belief that our climate commitments within the G20 must be aligned with the socio-economic aspirations of developing economies. In this conviction, Abhay Thakur and Ashish Sinha played critical roles, supported by a dedicated team of young policy specialists. Among them was Prabhat Upadhyaya, a standout Senior Policy Specialist whose deep understanding of climate negotiations and G20 experience significantly strengthened our position.

Throughout this journey, I must credit PM Modi, whose global diplomatic ties proved instrumental. His leadership on climate issues enabled India's G20 presidency to present solutions that combined sustainable development and environmental stewardship. Together, we rallied nations—developed and developing alike—on the path of green development, achieving outcomes we once thought were completely unattainable.

FIVE

GEOPOLITICS: THE ELEPHANT IN THE ROOM

Fifty-five kilometres from Delhi, in the heart of Nuh district in Haryana, the clock struck midnight. For the better part of several days and nights, the world's most influential diplomats had been locked in intense negotiations in the secluded Chola Villa of ITC Grand Bharat.

It was now midnight on 8 September 2023, and the fourth Sherpa meeting was ending. The G20 leaders had arrived in New Delhi, and the final G20 Summit was set to begin at 9 a.m. the next day, 9 September. Sixteen drafts had failed by 8 September, and I had to report back to PM Modi about our success or failure in negotiating one of the most hotly contested multilateral documents in India's diplomatic history. The clock was ticking, and the weight of our nation's expectations bore heavily on us.

My colleagues J.S. Nagaraj and Eenam and I had been at the heart of these negotiations, pushing for consensus on the most complex issues in a setting where every letter, every word, and every decision carried global significance.

Throughout this high-pressure, diplomatic showdown, our team worked tirelessly to bridge gaps, find common ground, and secure consensus amid a complex web of geopolitics, relating to the Russia-Ukraine conflict. Our mission was clear: India had to uphold its ability to straddle multiple blocs—G7, the Global South, Russia and China—to achieve consensus. We couldn't afford to let our voices be drowned out or sidelined. Failure was not an option, but in many uncertain moments during India's presidency, it seemed inevitable.

Caught in the geopolitical struggle between the G7 on one side, and Russia and China on the other, India's position was both precarious and pivotal. We had to walk a careful tightrope, navigating the country's red lines while making sure that we never lost sight of our ability to bring everyone together. We realized that if the emerging markets worked together, they would be a very potent force. Together with Brazil, South Africa, Indonesia and all other emerging markets, including Mexico, Argentina, Saudi Arabia and Türkiye, we allied with developing countries that stood firm in their united purpose.

▪

Divided House at Bali

A little over a year ago, the 2022 G20 Summit in Bali got off to a turbulent start when Russian Foreign Minister Sergey Lavrov was reportedly hospitalized shortly after his arrival. Although Russia denied these claims, insisting that he was merely undergoing a routine health check-up, the incident added pressure on the already tense atmosphere surrounding the negotiations. The controversies surrounding his health cast a shadow over Russia's participation and further complicated discussions amongst the world's leading economies.

In the wake of these events, the mood in Russia changed. The Russian media portrayed the negotiations as inherently biased, arguing that the blame was being disproportionately placed on their shoulders due to Lavrov's hospitalization. Russian officials voiced their frustration over what they perceived as a lack of acknowledgement regarding NATO's eastward expansion—an issue they viewed as critical to the prevailing tensions. Without proper references to their security concerns and an absence of genuine buy-in from Moscow, they felt that the geopolitical paragraph would not gain traction as a viable agreement beyond Bali. As the negotiations stalled, the reservations expressed by Russia became even more pronounced, emphasizing the difficulty of reaching a consensus in such a charged environment—especially a consensus that would last beyond the short term.

On 16 November, the G20 reached a precarious consensus through a split paragraph in the Bali Declaration. The effectively

Prime Minister Narendra Modi arrives for the New Delhi Leaders' Summit at Bharat Mandapam, New Delhi, in September 2023.

Presidency of healing, harmony, and hope: Prime Minister Modi takes over the ceremonial gavel from Joko Widodo, President of Indonesia, during the G20 Leaders' Summit in Bali in November 2022.

Prime Minister Modi hands over the ceremonial gavel to President Lula da Silva of Brazil at the conclusion of the G20 Leaders' Summit.

G20 becomes G21: Azali Assoumani, the chair of the African Union in 2023, embraces PM Modi as the African Union is formally inducted into the G20 as a permanent member under India's presidency.

US President Joe Biden, President of India Droupadi Murmu and Prime Minister of India Narendra Modi at the dinner hosted for G20 Leaders in New Delhi.

Collective vision for a harmonious world: Prime Minister Modi welcomes US President Joe Biden and other world leaders to Rajghat on the final day of India's G20 presidency.

Prime Minister Narendra Modi, US President Joe Biden, Brazilian President Luiz Inacio Lula da Silva, and South African President Cyril Ramaphosa along with Ajay Banga, President of the World Bank, during the New Delhi Leaders' Summit.

Redefining trade routes and charting a new era of connectivity! At the G20 New Delhi Summit, Prime Minister Modi brought global leaders together to unveil the groundbreaking India-Middle East-Europe Economic Corridor—an ambitious initiative that promises to redefine trade, foster innovation, and connect continents. Also seen are (from left): Prime Minister of Italy Giorgia Meloni, President of the European Commission Ursula von der Leyen, Saudi Arabian Crown Prince Mohammed bin Salman Al Saud, US President Joe Biden, and President of UAE, Sheikh Mohamed bin Zayed Al Nahyan.

Forging a sustainable future together: At the G20 Leaders' Summit in New Delhi, PM Modi united global leaders to ignite the Global Biofuels Alliance—paving the way for a cleaner, greener planet. A historic moment of collaboration, innovation, and commitment to a sustainable tomorrow.

Vasudhaiva Kutumbakam: World leaders assemble at Bharat Mandapam for the New Delhi Leaders' Summit.

Team Bharat, led by Prime Minister Modi, celebrates the New Delhi Leaders' Declaration.

negotiated, diluted agreed language addressed the then-recent escalations in the Russia-Ukraine conflict and its fallout. Paragraphs 3 and 4—the elephant in the room—had been arrived at through the tireless cooperation and collective efforts of emerging market economies within the G20, who understood the stakes of a joint communique for low- and middle-income countries. Alongside my counterparts in the Global South, I collaborated closely with Indonesia's Sherpa Dian Triansyah Djani to stitch together a declaration and preamble that would resonate with a global call for peace, while preserving the unique needs of the most vulnerable populations. In this declaration, the G20 leaders unanimously endorsed PM Modi's resounding message to Russian President Vladimir Putin on the sidelines of the Shanghai Cooperation Organization (SCO) in Samarkand, Uzbekistan, earlier that year, that 'today's era must not be of war.'[1]

> '3. This year, we have also witnessed the war in Ukraine further adversely impact the global economy. There was a discussion on the issue. We reiterated our national positions as expressed in other fora, including the UN Security Council and the UN General Assembly, which, in Resolution No. ES-11/1 dated 2 March 2022, as adopted by majority vote (141 votes for, 5 against, 35 abstentions, 12 absent) deplores in the strongest terms the aggression by the Russian Federation against Ukraine and demands its complete and unconditional withdrawal from the territory of Ukraine. Most members strongly condemned the war in Ukraine and stressed it is causing immense human suffering and exacerbating existing fragilities in the global economy –

[1]Haidar, Suhasini, 'PM Modi tells Vladimir Putin "now is not an era of war"', *The Hindu*, 17 September 2022, https://tinyurl.com/mv7w38at. Accessed on 8 September 2024.

> constraining growth, increasing inflation, disrupting supply chains, heightening energy and food insecurity, and elevating financial stability risks. There were other views and different assessments of the situation and sanctions. Recognizing that the G20 is not the forum to resolve security issues, we acknowledge that security issues can have significant consequences for the global economy.'
>
> '4. It is essential to uphold international law and the multilateral system that safeguards peace and stability. This includes defending all the Purposes and Principles enshrined in the Charter of the United Nations and adhering to international humanitarian law, including the protection of civilians and infrastructure in armed conflicts. The use or threat of use of nuclear weapons is inadmissible. The peaceful resolution of conflicts, efforts to address crises, as well as diplomacy and dialogue, are vital. Today's era must not be of war.'[2]

We thought the same language would hold during India's G20 presidency, but a little over five months later, this language failed at India's first-ever G20 Finance Ministers and Central Bank Governors (FMCBG) meeting in late February 2023 in Bengaluru.

Russia and China had changed their minds about the agreed language of paragraphs 3 and 4 of the Bali Declaration, arguing that geopolitical issues had no place for discussion at the G20 (China) and that the language of the paragraph did not accurately portray the varying interpretations of the situation by different countries (Russia). Russia also argued that this paragraph should be reserved for the Leaders' Declaration and not be used for

---

[2] 'G20 Bali Leaders' Declaration', Bali, Indonesia, 15-16 November 2022, https://tinyurl.com/5aams5au. Accessed on 8 September 2024.

ministerials. As a result, no Joint Communique—a document unanimously supported and endorsed by all G20 members—was adopted at the first ministerial meeting. Instead, the first FMCBG meeting produced a 'Chair's Summary and Outcome Document'.

Less than a week later, Dr Jaishankar chaired a supercharged meeting of foreign ministers in New Delhi, where US Secretary of State Antony Blinken and Russian Foreign Minister Sergey Lavrov sat in the same room for the first time since July 2022. The last time these diplomats came face to face was in Bali in 2022.

It is hard to describe the tension in the air without resorting to clichés, so let me just say—you could cut it with a knife. The looming spectre of war in Europe had moved from the quiet corner of the room to centre stage as the US and its G7 allies took every opportunity to condemn Russia's military action in Ukraine. Outside, in the relatively quiet corridors where media and logistics teams were waiting, the television suddenly switched on. On the screen was British Foreign Secretary James Cleverly, who was seen emphatically criticizing Russia for what he called 'President Vladimir Putin's military campaign against Ukraine.' Before the journalists could scramble to switch on their cameras, the feed was cut.

We were a long way from Bali 2022. The script had shifted.

Behind the closed doors of the meeting room, Russia doubled down on its position to reject paragraphs 3 and 4 of the text and confronted G7 head-on by pointing to the Nord Stream pipeline explosions and Ukrainian President Volodymyr Zelenskyy's admission that he never intended to implement the

Minsk Agreements with Russia.[3,4] 'The Bali Declaration took place half a year ago. A lot of events took place since then,' Lavrov later told the media, just as the Russian foreign ministry released a statement saying: 'A unanimous rejection was expressed of attempts to interfere in the internal affairs of other countries, to impose unilateral approaches through blackmail and threats, and to oppose the democratization of international relations.'[5, 6]

'The destructive policy of the US and its allies has already put the world on the brink of a disaster,' the statement added, which starkly underscored the profound ideological and practical chasm between Russia and China on the one hand, and the US and its allies on the other.[7]

On the other hand, Secretary Blinken urged China not to supply arms to Russia.[8] It became increasingly clear that India would have

---

[3]In September 2022, underwater explosions damaged Nord Stream 1 and 2 pipelines, leading to a gas leak in the Baltic Sea near Denmark. This incident, coupled with earlier disputes over the Ukraine war, resulted in the shutdown of Nord Stream 1 and the cancellation of the newly completed Nord Stream 2 project, which had faced opposition from Ukraine, the US, and Eastern European nations due to concerns about Russia's influence on Germany's energy security. Russia suspects US involvement in this sabotage.

'Nord Stream Sabotage One Year on: What to Know About the Attack', *Al Jazeera,* 23 September 2023, https://tinyurl.com/ms4dawzs. Accessed on 8 September 2024.

[4]Sharma, Rakshit, 'Zelenskyy takes credit for derailing Minsk Agreement meant to establish peace in eastern Ukraine', *Firstpost,* 10 February 2023, https://tinyurl.com/yre7v6k9. Accessed on 8 September 2024.

[5]Haidar, Suhasini, and Kallol Bhattacherjee, 'G20 Foreign Ministers Meeting | Divisions between Western countries, Russia-China derail joint statement', *The Hindu,* 3 March 2023, https://tinyurl.com/2s4mynsn. Accessed on 8 September 2024.

[6]Agence France-Presse, 'Russia condemns Western 'blackmail, threats' at G20', *Firstpost,* 2 March 2023, https://tinyurl.com/w7mar828. Accessed on 8 September 2024.

[7]Ibid.

[8]'Secretary Antony J. Blinken at a Press Availability', US Department of State,

to pivot its tactics quickly at G20 to avoid a permanently divided house. We decided to be extremely ambitious on development issues and put them at the centre stage during our negotiation while leaving geopolitics for later.

On cue, the G20 Meeting of Agricultural Chief Scientists (MACS) in Varanasi on 19 April failed to reach a consensus and also produced a Chair's Summary, which states 'Paragraphs 3 and 4 of this document, as taken from the G20 Bali Leaders' Declaration (15 to 16 November 2022), were agreed to by all member countries except Russia and China.'[9]

Something had to be done and done fast. Fuelled by a sense of urgency, we sprang into action, fully aware that allowing this situation to persist until the end was not an option. With a well-established rapport with the other Sherpas, especially those from emerging market economies, I initiated direct contact and was determined to push through the necessary changes to the Bali paragraphs and their implications. The month of May was relatively quiet in terms of ministerial meetings, and we used this time to calibrate our next steps as a team.

In a personal letter sent to all Sherpas on 6 June, I emphasized that 'a mere Chair Summary as the outcome document at the Development Ministerial is not what India's G20 presidency seeks,' making it abundantly clear that 'my leader has directed me to convince all G20 countries that we need to work for a consensus so that key developmental challenges are addressed.' All Sherpas needed to understand the responsibility before us. As representatives of our countries in the world's foremost multilateral forum, I told them that 'we cannot afford to repeatedly demonstrate the G20 as a divided grouping.' This message underscored the critical

2 March 2023, https://tinyurl.com/3yy65wm9. Accessed on 8 September 2024.
[9]G20 Meeting of Agricultural Chief Scientists (MACS), Varanasi, India, 17–19 April 2023, 'Chair's Summary & Outcome Document', https://tinyurl.com/munuh25e. Accessed on 8 September 2024.

need for cohesion within the grouping, as repeated failure would be 'a challenge to the credibility of the G20.' 'We cannot fail the planet. We cannot fail its people. And we cannot fail for our common future,' I wrote, adding, "We need to find an interim solution that can enable the G20 Ministerials to adopt ambitious and consensus-based outcomes, while the Sherpa Track continues to keep working for finding a common landing for the Leader's Summit in September this year.'

With the vital Development Ministers Meeting days away, I convened a virtual meeting with all G20 Sherpas on 7 June, to take them through permutations of agreed and suggested language that we hoped would strike a balance between contradictory country positions. My peers needed to enter this discussion with a renewed sense of purpose. The cracks in contemporary multilateralism were revealing themselves across platforms worldwide, and PM Modi was determined to use India's presidency to revitalize efforts toward global cooperation. As his emissary, I felt compelled to address the pressing issue of G20 unity.

We presented three different options for paragraphs 3 and 4 during this virtual convening. Despite echoing the recently agreed language on the Ukraine crisis in the Hiroshima Action Statement for Resilient Global Food Security[10]—signed by the G7 and its partners on 20 May 2023—there was no progress. The G7 insisted on holding Russia to account and, to our surprise, we saw certain emerging economies also swing support in their direction. We had reached yet another stalemate.

---

[10]The Hiroshima Action Statement for Resilient Global Food Security was signed by Japan, Australia, Brazil, Canada, Comoros, the Cook Islands, France, Germany, India, Indonesia, Italy, the Republic of Korea, the UK, the US, Vietnam and the EU.

'Hiroshima Action Statement for Resilient Global Food Security', Ministry of External Affairs, Government of India, 20 May 2023, https://tinyurl.com/mcxex6zd. Accessed on 8 September 2024.

The G7 had some heavy hitters in its midst, each bringing their weight and perspective to the negotiations. Among them, Tim Barrow, the former British Ambassador to Russia, brought a keen intelligence background in his role as the British Sherpa. His meticulous approach to drafting, combined with a deep understanding of Russia, allowed him to adeptly switch between flexibility and firmness. This made him invaluable for strategic insights, although it also posed some challenges in terms of bringing him around.

On the same table sat Germany's Sherpa, Dr Jörg Kukies. An economist, Jörg brought a calm, methodical presence to the discussions. He didn't hesitate to voice his strong condemnation of Russia's actions, yet he was careful to remind everyone that the G20 must play a pivotal role. His emphasis on the need for multilateral negotiations highlighted the many overlapping relationships at play. Unlike the bilateral strategies we often employed, Jörg's systematic all-hands-on-deck approach revealed the challenges we faced in navigating such a diverse group.

Together, these representatives shaped an environment where collaboration was necessary, but the path ahead was anything but straightforward.

On 12 June, Dr Jaishankar did everything in his power to steer discussions away from geopolitical issues during the DMM in Varanasi. The divided factions were unrelenting, and Dr Jaishankar stood firm on India's right to decide the footnotes of objection. The EAM truthfully recorded Russia's decision to disassociate itself from the status of this document as a common outcome because of the references to paragraphs 10 and 11 (erstwhile paras 3 and 4). India also reflected China's position clearly, which stated that 'the meeting outcome should not include any reference to the Ukraine crisis.'[11]

[11]Varanasi Development Ministerial Outcome Document & Chair's Summary, Varanasi, Uttar Pradesh, 12 June 2023, https://tinyurl.com/2zrhv39c. Accessed on 8 September 2024.

India quickly recognized that a firm stand was needed if we had to prevent substantive outcomes from getting undone by geopolitical skirmishes. At the DMM, the term Outcome Document and Chair's Summary (ODCS) was coined to emphasize the agreements reached rather than the disagreements. There was substantial consensus on a wide range of development issues, and we believed the terminology used to refer to the document should reflect this. All meetings had a comprehensive Outcome Document that highlighted these developmental agreements, and only the geopolitical paragraphs that eluded consensus comprised the Chair's Summary. From that day on, we refused to be held hostage by the concerns of the handful at the cost of the needful. We resolved to refocus the G20 on its developmental mission.

Thereafter, the G20 Agriculture Ministers' Meeting on 17 June, the Tourism Ministerial on 21 June, the Education Ministerial on 22 June, the Research (RIIG) Ministerial on 5 July, and the third FMCBG on 18 July, all followed the DMM Model, resulting in an ODCS.

Push and Pulls of International Diplomacy

In June, we quietly began direct negotiations with Russia, led by Nagaraj alongside Russia's Sous-Sherpa Marat Berdyev, who was under the direct supervision of Alexander Pankin, Deputy Minister of Foreign Affairs of the Russian Federation. This back channel was crucial in understanding how far Russia will compromise. It allowed us to clearly identify Russia's red lines, providing valuable insights on how to balance competing interests as we began our negotiations with the US.

Just as India's top diplomats continued to work tirelessly behind the scenes to find a middle ground between Russia and the US, a defining moment in the G20 presidency came when

Sergey Lavrov penned a letter to Dr Jaishankar. This letter exposed the deepening rift between the Western bloc and Russia, underscoring the challenges that threatened to unravel the G20's delicate consensus-based negotiations.

In his letter, Lavrov articulated his concern that the G20 negotiation processes were veering into the realm of geopolitics and confrontational bloc politics. He bemoaned the relentless efforts of Western powers to introduce the 'Ukrainian paragraph' into the G20 discussions by 'actively using methods of pressure and blackmail,' stressing that this move was 'contrary to the economic mandate of the forum and the principle of consensus.' Lavrov's letter, both a plea and a warning, hinted at the widening schism in the G20, exacerbated by conflicting interpretations of the Ukrainian conflict and the crippling effects of sanctions.

In the same letter, the Russians shared their suggested phrasing for the final Leaders' Declaration. However, the suggestions were untenable with references to conflicts in the Middle East and other attacks on Russia's domestic infrastructure like the Nord Stream gas pipelines and the Kakhovka hydroelectric power plant, which the other G20 countries would never agree to.

Meanwhile, China maintained that political issues were not within the mandate of the ministerials, and should not be discussed at all in the working groups.

On the same day, Lavrov met in Moscow with the ambassadors of G20's global majority countries: Argentina, Brazil, China, India, Indonesia, Mexico, Saudi Arabia, South Africa and Türkiye. The Russians converged on one central theme: the imperative to depoliticize the G20's negotiation processes and activities. They advocated for focusing the discussions on the social and economic challenges and needs of the Global South. Lavrov emphasized the ideals of democratizing global governance and pursuing the SDGs, all while stressing the pivotal role of dynamically developing economies in trade, industry and finance.

The push and pull of international diplomacy are many. During our presidency, we truly learned what it means to be caught between an immovable object and an unstoppable force. Our team, determined to find a kink in the armour, finally made ground on 21 July during the Labour and Employment Ministerial in Indore. It was a pivotal moment when Russia—as a result of the backchannel negotiations on the Ukraine paragraphs and the footnotes of the various ministerials—agreed to the text of the principles outlined in paragraph 4. Russia acknowledged the document as a Chair's Summary *only* because it maintained its stance on paragraph 3, citing concerns about language, which it saw as a condemnation of their country from the UN perspective.

At this stage, Russia had also fully agreed to paragraph 4.

A few weeks later, Russia's stance softened a little more. The footnote shifted the focus from the document being a Chair Summary to Russia's specific disassociation from Paragraph 11(i) (i.e., Bali para 3) 'due to its distinct view on the issue and from a few definitions in the text.'

Our negotiations were a continuous endeavour, a constant striving for improvement. From meeting to meeting, we witnessed Russia's position evolve favourably as we persisted in our diplomatic efforts. This pattern was repeated at the Anti-Corruption Ministerial in Kolkata on 12 August, where we encountered the same old ODCS with its familiar footnote. On 19 August, during the Digital Economy Ministers' Meeting in Bengaluru, the language of Russia expressing 'agreement with the rest of the text' entered the G20 lexicon, with the country reserving their stance only on Paragraph 3. At the parallel Health Ministerial in Gandhinagar on the same day, and a short six days later during the Trade and Investment talks in Jaipur, we followed a similar formula.

The challenge lay in addressing Paragraph 3 to ensure Russia's buy-in. Recognizing this necessity, we embarked on an independent drafting process. After producing a draft, we conducted a detailed analysis of Russia's suggestions, realizing it was time to abandon the Bali formulation.

This moment in multilateralism needed something new—an Indian version.

At this juncture, I had another discussion with PM Modi and Dr Jaishankar, and their counsel resonated with the idea of crafting a new paragraph highlighting the Indian perspective and showcasing India's adeptness in bringing everyone together under a common purpose.

Multilateralism: The Indian Way

The negotiations with Russia, China and the US, which I led with the support of dedicated diplomats Nagaraj and Eenam, were in full swing, and we knew that this final month leading up to the summit would be marked by relentless diplomatic efforts.

Nagaraj, a seasoned diplomat who was the Chef de Cabinet to the President of the 76th Session of the United Nations General Assembly (UNGA), brought a wealth of diplomatic expertise and remarkable drafting skills to the team. His meticulous approach and adept negotiation tactics played a pivotal role in navigating the complex nuances of the discussions.

Eenam, who also had a wealth of experience in international diplomacy, was another driving force in the negotiations. Her enthusiasm, knowledge of the UN, and passion made her an invaluable asset during these intense diplomatic exchanges. She understood the nuances of India's position on substantive policy issues extremely well. I often relied on Nagaraj and Eenam to navigate the finer details of disagreements.

The intensity of the negotiations was such that, in one instance, Nagaraj found himself in a fierce argument with the French Sherpa Emmanuel Bonne. He defended India's draft so vehemently that Bonne got up angrily and left the room, clarifying that he would only discuss matters with me. This, too, was a strategy. As the antithesis of Nagaraj's bad cop, I could extend an olive branch to him and smooth things over as the good cop.

This yin-yang strategy of assertiveness and appeasement not only reflected our playbook but was mirrored across countries, each honing their tactics in positing their national interests.

The US exemplified this strategy with Sous-Sherpa Christina Segal-Knowles as the ruthless bad cop, complementing Sherpa Mike Pyle's amiable approach. Their coordinated efforts leveraged pressure and persuasion, extracting favourable terms for the US. Then there was Canada's Sherpa Christopher MacLennan, who stood out as a clear-thinking economist and advisor to PM Justin Trudeau. Despite the tensions that had characterized India-Canada relations, Christopher remained positive and constructive, willing to engage in open dialogue. While he often made strong points on bilateral matters, it was clear he was committed to finding common ground.

Across the table, Bjoern Seibert played a significant role as the Sherpa for the EU. His close ties with the EU President and our strong personal rapport allowed him to balance assertiveness and diplomacy, ensuring cohesive and effective negotiations. This duality was essential, as each nation wished to maximize gains while maintaining diplomatic relations.

Each country, driven by its national interests, tried to secure the best possible outcomes, creating a pressure-cooker environment. This 20-way tug-of-war resembled a delicate spider's web, where each strand tugged at risked creating ripples throughout the structure and jeopardizing the very fabric of our collaborative efforts.

We often relied on this push-and-pull dynamic in the thorniest of moments. Throughout these interactions, however, our commitment to representing the interests of emerging markets and reaching consensus remained unwavering.

We failed several times, but each time we were able to quickly come up with an alternate revised draft.

Before our impending final rounds of negotiations, I wanted to take the US into confidence. A draft had been shared with them informally and inputs were sought from Christina. An exceptionally tough and unyielding negotiator, her contributions highlighted the grave global repercussions stemming from the ongoing conflict in Ukraine, particularly its ramifications on food security, rising energy costs and disrupted supply chains, focusing on the suffering that exists particularly in developing and least developed countries. Through her perspective, the redlines for the US became clear.

Even before we shared the draft with the US, we had multiple video conferences with the Russian negotiators to determine the acceptable terms and identify any non-negotiable points. Finally, once Pankin signed off, we knew both the minimalist and the maximalist positions of the Russian side.

We were days away from the last Sherpa meeting—the final opportunity before the New Delhi Summit to galvanize consensus on the draft NDLD. Multiple permutations of language had been considered, but we were hitting dead ends. While we had been working with Russia all year to negotiate acceptable phrasing and get them fully on board, I realized that the other half of the equation—the US—fully needed to be brought into the fold. They had previously written to us that the draft in its current form still contained 'several Russian poison pills'.

On 27 August, I reached out to Mike Pyle via a letter in which I underscored that we aimed to maintain the credibility of the

G20, a forum that must stand as a beacon of global cooperation. The contentious issue of the Bali paras, where Russia had insisted on incorporating lengthy text on incidents unrelated to the G20's purview, had been a longstanding point of disagreement. It was now 'our clear assessment [...] that we will not be able to achieve success on the Bali paras.'

Mike, to his credit, was always positive and constructive, focused on finding solutions rather than dwelling on the problem. He believed in India's success, partly due to the strong relationship between PM Modi and President Joe Biden. His background in the private sector was evident in his pragmatic approach, and he worked seamlessly with his Sous-Sherpa Christina to draft key Finance Track paragraphs on climate change and multilateral reforms.

I knew I could be forthright with him, so my communication was clear: the discussions surrounding geopolitical issues were complex and the text was a sensitive matter. I acknowledged that it was critical to address all concerns, but we also needed to ensure that the language didn't veer into unrelated matters or deviate from the G20's focus areas. The intricacies of this negotiation had brought us to a point where a decisive strategy was imperative.

With diplomacy hanging in the balance, I shared that we had reviewed various inputs, including those of the US, and had also scrutinized the language of the Hiroshima plus partners. Our new draft would go beyond this text. It was time to explore new, more robust options—an Indian version of the paragraphs on geopolitical issues.

Shortly before the last Sherpa meeting, I met PM Modi. His message was unequivocal: consensus at all costs, otherwise India should think of other options. He entrusted the processes to us and was only interested in the outcome.

Villa without a Verdict

On 3 September, the G20 India team entered the fourth and final Sherpa meeting in New Delhi with an equal mix of resolve and determination. All efforts to reach a full consensus had failed over the last nine months—India's presidency had not been able to produce a Joint Communiqué for any one of its WGs. Internally, we were doubtful if the draft NDLD would pass. Our body language, however, remained positive and confident.

During the informal Sofa Talk with all the Sherpas at the ITC Grand Bharat in Manesar, it became evident that this wasn't going to be a congenial exchange of ideas but a showdown of contrasting viewpoints.[12] The arguments were heated, and contrarian perspectives clashed in a debate, filling the room with tension. As the debate raged on, it was clear that reaching a consensus on the contentious Russia-Ukraine geopolitical issue would be highly complex, if not an impossibility.

Russian Sherpa Svetlana Lukash was the most experienced Sherpa amongst us, persuasive and knowledgeable in geopolitical affairs. Despite the looming context of incompatible geopolitical positions, she remained cheerful and friendly, working tirelessly for Russia's interests. Even at the Bali summit, where no G7 leader was willing to engage with or be photographed with her, she continued to advocate for Russia's interests. Her Sous-Sherpa, Marat Berdyev, was a difficult negotiator, presenting Russia's complex scenarios with a nationalist perspective that was hard to shake. At the end of the presidency, Svetlana conveyed her deep respect and heartfelt gratitude, highlighting a strong personal and professional bond.

By the end of Day 1 at Manesar, it became clear that while achieving consensus on development issues was necessary, it was

[12]Sofa Talks is an informal meeting between the Sherpas to discuss the delivery of the preparatory document for the summit.

not enough. We realized that addressing the geopolitical context was essential for our collective success. Recognizing the need for a different approach, a collective decision was taken to transition from discussions to action on the draft.

At midnight later that day, after splitting hair over the subtleties of semantics, I led all the diplomatic teams into the drafting room in the Chola Villa, where the suite's twenty television screens (one for each Sherpa) displayed various versions of greened and red text. This was our command centre, and it was within the closed walls of this room that the nitty-gritty of diplomacy would unfold.

Our collective anxiety had reached a tipping point. We were acutely aware of the media's watchful eyes, with rumours circulating about the status of our talks. The prospect of the text being leaked would derail whatever progress we had made so far. To mitigate this risk, no mobile phones were allowed, and not a single version of a working draft would be circulated in paper to avoid the possibility of even one confidential photograph or piece of text being leaked to the media.

Everything was to be handled through a single laptop. Each Sherpa was summoned individually to discuss the contentious paragraphs. Every adjustment to the text was made behind tightly closed doors, with the weight of our collective ambitions resting on this one device.

A sense of foreboding was palpable, and the shadow of imminent failure loomed large over our efforts. At this stage, everyone was certain that the New Delhi Summit was a write-off.

Failure for India would have resulted in extreme embarrassment. As the most populous country in the world, with the Global South depending on us and our ambitious proclamations about reshaping the multilateral order, we faced significant pressure. Without a guiding framework to direct the discussions, we risked being lost amid what each country assumed was an irrefutable political position. We needed something to unite us when our geopolitical aims seemed to be fundamentally at odds with each other.

I asked my team to put up a blank page on the main screen, on which I began drafting a set of principles—15 of them—to serve as the foundation for the negotiations. Introducing these guiding principles opened a new, albeit cautious, pathway. The path remained challenging, yet the collective determination to work towards a solution instilled a sense of possibility amidst the uncertainty.

The fifteen principles were:

1. Concerning the war in Ukraine and recalling the discussions in Bali, all members shall refrain in their international relations from threat or use of force against the territorial integrity or political independence of any state.
2. All states will act in a manner consistent with the Purposes and Principles of the UN Charter in its entirety.
3. We reiterate our national positions and resolutions adopted at the UN Security Council and the UN General Assembly.
4. We note with deep concern the adverse impact of the war on food and energy security, supply chains, and global macro-financial stability and growth.
5. We note with concern that the war is adding to an already complicated policy environment for countries still recovering from the COVID-19 pandemic and the economic disruption which has derailed progress towards the SDGs.
6. We call for unimpeded deliveries of grain, food and fertilizer to prevent global food insecurity.
7. We call for the full and effective implementation of

the MoU between the Russian Federation and the Secretariat of the United Nations on promoting Russian food products and fertilizers to the world markets, and the initiative on the safe transportation of grains and foodstuffs from Ukrainian Ports (BSI) by bringing Ukrainian grain and foodstuffs and Russian food products and fertilizers to the world markets.

8. This is necessary to meet the demand in developing and least developed countries, particularly in Africa.
9. It is essential to uphold international law and the multilateral system that safeguards peace and stability.
10. We will defend all the Purposes and Principles enshrined in the Charter of the UN and adhere to international humanitarian law, including the protection of civilians and infrastructure in armed conflicts.
11. The use or threat of use of nuclear weapons is inadmissible.
12. The peaceful resolution of conflicts and efforts to address crises as well as engage in diplomacy and dialogue are critical.
13. Today's era must not be of war.
14. Recognizing that while the G20 is not the forum to resolve geopolitical issues, we acknowledge that security issues can have significant consequences for the global economy.
15. We will unite in our tireless endeavour to support all initiatives that support a just and durable peace based on respect for sovereign equality of all states, and international law.

These principles were crafted to guide our approach to addressing pressing global challenges while fostering consensus among member states. By emphasizing the importance of refraining from threat or use of force and acting under the UN Charter, we created a sound foundation for respectful and cooperative international relations. Our recognition of the adverse impacts of the war in Ukraine—particularly on food and energy security, supply chains, and economic growth in the ongoing recovery from the COVID-19 pandemic—highlighted the urgent need for joint action.

We called for unimpeded delivery of essential goods like grain and fertilizers, particularly for developing countries in Africa, to combat global food insecurity. Our commitment to uphold international law and prioritize peaceful conflict resolution underscored the need for dialogue and diplomacy. While acknowledging that the G20 may not directly resolve geopolitical disputes, we recognized that security issues could significantly affect the global economy. Ultimately, these principles served as a cohesive framework that not only guided our discussions but also led to a shared commitment among members to pursue a just and lasting peace based on mutual respect and cooperation.

On seeing these 15 principles, delegates from various nations recognized India's commitment to impartiality and fairness, seeking a resolution based on principled considerations. This realization prompted swift action, with the US taking the lead, followed by the active involvement of the G7 countries, all developing countries, as well as China and Russia. Each brought their unique perspectives and priorities to the table, giving birth to several sets of principles based on their respective needs and expectations.

However, the journey from the principles to the final draft of the NDLD was far from smooth. The text continued to face constant revisions and objections after 300 hours of negotiations over 250 bilateral meetings. The weight and seriousness of the negotiations were felt by all participants, but the pursuit of a mutually agreeable outcome still seemed far from reach.

PM Modi was acutely aware of the stakes involved. He had asked me to send him urgent situation reports every two hours, a task that demanded immense multitasking and quick analysis. This constant communication kept PM Modi informed, but also spurred us into action, helping us map out the negotiations and take stock of our progress. It allowed us to see the bigger picture and identify where the pieces of the puzzle could fit together.

I was reminded of the times I had to make multiple presentations to him as CEO of NITI Aayog during initiatives like Startup India and Make in India. Until the concepts were crystal clear and the implementation plans were foolproof, he did not give his go-ahead. PM Modi has always cultivated a culture of thorough preparation and execution in the initiatives he has led, and he expected no less from the G20 India team. His hands-on approach at this crucial hour was the stimulus we needed to push through obstacles and drive meaningful progress—proving once again that when the leader engages directly, the entire team rallies to deliver results.

Throughout this intricate process, the emerging markets played a pivotal role, and they stood like a rock with India. Their unity was a priority and I, together with Brazilian Sherpa Mauricio Carvalho Lyrio and South African Sherpa Zane Dangor, left no stone unturned in maintaining this alliance. Mauricio was a strong supporter of the emerging markets alliance, and together with Zane's pragmatic approach, they were invaluable in the negotiations. Both diplomats brought their unique strengths to the table—Mauricio's distinguished diplomatic career and Zane's profound knowledge of international law and the UN provided the intellectual heft needed to hold our ground.

Indonesia's Sherpa Djani had vast geopolitical experience but was regrettably pulled away for ASEAN duties. We therefore needed to collaborate with South Africa and Brazil, bringing together all emerging markets, including Turkey, Saudi Arabia, Argentina and Mexico, among others.

The diverse personalities of the Sherpas from these nations complemented each other like pieces of a complex puzzle, each adding a critical dimension to our collective efforts. Jorge Argüello, Argentina's Ambassador in Washington and G20 Sherpa, was a spirited advocate who infused discussions with a vibrant Latin American perspective. A keen ability to connect on a personal level matched his unwavering support for emerging markets, fostering camaraderie among the representatives.

In contrast, Türkiye Sherpa Raci Kaya brought an unconventional approach to the table. While his background was not rooted in diplomacy, his knack for navigating challenging discussions was impressive. Raci's positivity and sincere desire for collective success were clear in every discussion, making it easier to tackle critical issues like gender, climate and energy.

Meanwhile, Mexico's contributions were amplified by Sherpa Carmen Moreno Toscano and Sous-Sherpa Jennifer Feller. Carmen was known for her analytical rigour, putting Mexico's interests at the forefront of the negotiations. Coupled with Jennifer's collaborative spirit and exceptional communication skills, they helped align Mexico's positions with the broader emerging market group.

As a unit, the Sherpas of the Global South enriched the negotiations, enhancing the effectiveness and cohesion of our discussions and propelling us toward a unified stance on pressing global challenges.

As the drafts kept evolving, we had to repeatedly find ways to circumvent every country's set of red lines and non-negotiables. Even within the G7, the divergence of red lines was unmistakable, sometimes even in direct contradiction. For example, the French Sherpa held a distinct perspective on the nuclear doctrine, while the Japanese delegation adamantly sought to retain the exact language used in the Bali paragraphs 3 and 4, i.e., '*The use or threat of use of nuclear weapons is inadmissible.*'

Japan Sherpa Keiichi Ono was very focused on reflecting PM Fumio Kishida's strong commitment to Japan's nuclear stance. Supportive and lively, he balanced Japan's G7 leadership with the broader G20 agenda. While he would have liked to focus solely on the G7, he realized that the G20 negotiations, which included Russia and China, presented unique challenges and were far more complicated than the G7, which Japan was leading.

Through these tense and constructive deliberations, we had reached a consensus on all other paragraphs of the Declaration, including contentious positions around climate and energy. But after several relentless days and sleepless nights, during which we had exchanged over 16 drafts of agreed and newly constructed language, we were still at an impasse. The Chola Villa had failed to reach a verdict.

The Final Gambit: 'Take it or Leave it'

By the afternoon of 8 September, the last Sherpa meeting had officially come to an end, but negotiations hadn't. The leaders and their delegations had started coming into Delhi, and the Sherpas wanted to brief their leaders. With less than 20 hours to go, we moved negotiations to the headquarters of the G20 Secretariat in Delhi, the Sushma Swaraj Bhawan.

With Brazilian Sherpa Lyrio and South African Sherpa Dangor, and a late inclusion of the Indonesian Sherpa Djani—who had returned from the 18th East Asia Summit in Jakarta—the final draft began to take shape, a draft that would serve as a litmus test for unity.

Just two days before India's G20 Summit, the ASEAN Summit in Jakarta had failed to achieve consensus on the crucial geopolitical paragraph, revealing significant fractures within this key regional bloc. ASEAN, which comprises ten member nations—Indonesia, Malaysia, the Philippines, Singapore, Thailand, Brunei, Vietnam, Laos, Myanmar and Cambodia—has long prided itself on promoting regional cooperation, consensus-led multilateral governance, and stability. However, the inability to address pressing security challenges, particularly concerning China's assertiveness and the ongoing crisis in Myanmar, illustrated a troubling decline in regional collaboration.

This failure was particularly striking given the escalating security dynamics in the region. As tensions mounted, the paralysis within ASEAN raised concerns about its effectiveness and relevance, amplifying the struggles we faced in our negotiations for the Delhi Declaration. The inability of ASEAN to respond coherently to such fundamental issues cast deeper doubts on our project to align the interests of the Global South. We needed a unified message more than ever, but each setback in global diplomacy served as a stark reminder of the obstacles we were likely to encounter. Dominoes were falling all around us—if smaller international bodies could not work, what hope did we have for the G20?

The atmosphere in the room was thick with negativity and pessimism. As the night wore on, a prevailing sense of doubt took hold; many believed that India would not be able to reach an agreement by morning. We hadn't even submitted a written draft until this point, leading to murmurs of frustration. It seemed we had pushed things too far and left the impossible for the end, when energies were spent, and faith in global diplomacy was at an all-time low.

Yet, despite the pervasive pessimism, we carried on with our drafting, determined to shift the narrative in our favour. It was an uphill battle, but as we pressed on, a faint glimmer of hope began to emerge.

At midnight on 9 September, the night before the G20 Summit, we assertively put our words on paper and presented a final written draft for the first time to all the Sherpas present at the Sushma Swaraj Bhawan. The draft was not only ambitious and forward-looking but also designed to address the concerns of all parties involved. Backed by the support of PM Modi, I made our stand clear: this draft was non-negotiable.

This was our final draft:[13]

For the Planet, People, Peace and Prosperity

7. We note with deep concern the immense human suffering and the adverse impact of wars and conflicts around the world.

8. Concerning the war in Ukraine, while recalling the discussion in Bali, we reiterated our national positions and resolutions adopted at the UN Security Council and the UN General Assembly (A/RES/ES-11/1 and A/RES/ES-11/6) and underscored that all states must act in a manner consistent with the Purposes and Principles of the UN Charter in its entirety. In line with the UN Charter, all states must refrain from the threat or use of force to seek territorial acquisition against the territorial integrity and sovereignty or political independence of any state. The use or threat of use of nuclear weapons is inadmissible.

9. Reaffirming that the G20 is the premier forum for international economic cooperation and recognizing that while the G20 is not the platform to resolve geopolitical and security issues, we acknowledge that these issues can have significant consequences for the global economy.

---

[13]'G20 New Delhi Leaders' Declaration', New Delhi, India, 9–10 September 2023, https://tinyurl.com/t6dzsa69. Accessed on 9 September 2024.

10. We highlighted the human suffering and negative added impacts of the war in Ukraine with regard to global food and energy security, supply chains, macro-financial stability, inflation, and growth, which has complicated the policy environment for countries, especially developing and least developed countries which are still recovering from the COVID-19 pandemic and the economic disruption which has derailed progress towards the SDGs. There were different views and assessments of the situation.

11. We appreciate the efforts of Türkiye and UN-brokered Istanbul Agreements consisting of the Memorandum of Understanding between the Russian Federation and the Secretariat of the United Nations on Promoting Russian Food Products and Fertilizers to the World Markets and the Initiative on the Safe Transportation of Grain and Foodstuffs from Ukrainian Ports (Black Sea Initiative) and call for their full, timely and effective implementation to ensure the immediate and unimpeded deliveries of grain, foodstuffs, and fertilizers/inputs from the Russian Federation and Ukraine. This is necessary to meet the demand in developing and least developed countries, particularly those in Africa.

12. In this context, emphasizing the importance of sustaining food and energy security, we called for the cessation of military destruction or other attacks on relevant infrastructure. We also expressed deep concern about the adverse impact that conflicts have on the security of civilians thereby exacerbating existing socio-economic fragilities and vulnerabilities and hindering an effective humanitarian response.

13. We call on all states to uphold the principles of international law including territorial integrity and

> sovereignty, international humanitarian law, and the multilateral system that safeguards peace and stability. The peaceful resolution of conflicts and efforts to address crises as well as diplomacy and dialogue are critical. We will unite in our endeavour to address the adverse impact of the war on the global economy and welcome all relevant and constructive initiatives that support a comprehensive, just, and durable peace in Ukraine that will uphold all the Purposes and Principles of the UN Charter for the promotion of peaceful, friendly, and good neighbourly relations among nations in the spirit of 'One Earth, One Family, One Future'.
>
> 14. Today's era must not be of war.

Not only was our judgement sound but it was also echoed by others. The Brazilian Sherpa had already discussed it with his president and saw it as a fair document. We had the full support of Saudi Arabia, Mexico, Argentina and Türkiye. Eight nations stood united behind this final draft. Together with Brazil, South Africa and Indonesia, we presented it as a common draft from the G20 Troika, or rather the Tetrad (group of 4), of developing countries.

Further, it had the approval of my PM, and his unequivocal support empowered me to say, 'Take it or leave it. There will be no more discussions, no more debates at the Sherpa level. If anyone has an objection, please ask your leader to take it up to my leader. For now, this text is greened.'

A risky move, some might say, but sometimes bold actions are needed. I emphasized that if this draft was rejected, India was ready to explore other avenues, and potentially work closely with BRICS and IBSA instead of a divided G20. I spoke with authority and conviction, highlighting the fact that my leader maintained personal one-on-one relationships with most of the other leaders. This connection not only strengthened our negotiating position but also fostered an atmosphere of trust, which was essential in these critical discussions.

I made my declaration and walked out of the room. This final meeting was brief yet intense, marked by India's resolute tone. My leader commanded global respect and his steadfast commitment to consensus empowered me to be gutsy and bold at crunch time.

As the morning sun rose, I awoke with a peaceful assurance. In the early hours of the day, I had already received a message from the EU, Germany, France, Italy and Japan that they agreed with our draft. Italian Sherpa Luca Ferrari had been a warm and friendly presence throughout the negotiations and represented the heart of Italian culture, which we hold very close to home in India. He often praised the hospitality at Sherpa meetings in India, calling them the best and most beautiful he had attended.

Just as a fleeting sense of calm settled at the G20 Secretariat, a critical figure stepped into the spotlight—Alexander Pankin. As Russia's key negotiator, Pankin, along with the Russian Sherpa, was in constant touch with Lavrov. They had been sent back with extreme and untenable additions proposed by Lavrov which led to clashes with the G7 nations and severely complicated our discussions.

Russia insisted on the inclusion of the word 'sanction'. This led to extensive discussions with Pankin, lasting for two and a half hours, to persuade them to reconsider. The stakes were high, as refusal to compromise would have left Russia isolated with a 19-1 vote against it. We finally had to tell Russia that this was not feasible and would not be accepted by other countries. We made it abundantly clear to Russia that its insistence on this matter put significant pressure on India and made it impossible for us to move forward.

Throughout the negotiations, the G7 countries were pressuring India to invite Ukrainian President, Volodymyr Zelenskyy. However, India's stance was to keep the guest list exclusive to the G20 leaders. In the previous instance in Bali, when Zelenskyy was invited by Indonesia, he dominated the meeting with a non-stop 25-minute virtual speech, effectively hijacking the event. On Dr Jaishankar's advice, I had to inform the Russian negotiator that if they didn't agree, the first speaker following PM Modi's speech would be Zelenskyy.

This bold and assertive negotiation tactic ultimately worked, and Russia relented.

Soon after, with barely an hour to go for the leaders' meeting, I spoke with the US Sherpa Pyle, who informed me that after discussions with his President, they were willing to accept the draft, but it was contingent on two conditions: a minor language change, and the prior approval from China and Russia. We had already managed to convince Russia. With Russia on board and the unanimous support of all G7 nations alongside emerging markets, we felt we were close to a breakthrough.

But even as we awaited the approval of two key players—the US and China—the latter posed a challenge.

The Chinese had consistently maintained that they had no problem with the draft as long as all emerging markets were in agreement. But at this penultimate stage, Li Kexin, the head of the Chinese team, raised an unexpected concern. He pointed out a bilateral challenge with the US, stemming from a greened portion of the G20 declaration that stated that the 2026 G20 Summit would be hosted in the US. The Chinese Sherpa explained that the US would not grant them visas, not even for their governor in Hong Kong. They would not agree to the geopolitical paras until they received a written guarantee that they would be issued visas.

At about 8:00 in the morning, PM Modi visited the Bharat Mandapam for an inspection before the start of the leaders' meeting. I was to brief him on our progress so far. When he enquired about the Leaders' Declaration, I outlined the conflict between the US and China and informed him that the NDLD was still not finalized. He paused for a moment, wondering as to why bilateral issues were being raised in a multilateral meeting, before replying that he did not want to get into the procedures or the process, but wanted to see the result—a consensus—very soon. He expected the Sherpa to navigate and secure the final agreement.

The leaders' meeting commenced at 9 a.m. I had to undertake parallel negotiations in a dedicated session from 9:30 to 11:30 a.m., in the room adjacent to the Leaders' Hall in the Bharat Mandapam. I, along with Pyle and Li, hammered out the details of the letter. We opted to use the term 'ensure' instead of 'guarantee'. By noon, we had successfully resolved this bilateral matter, even though technically it was beyond the scope of India's role as G20 Chair.

With China's consent, and both of America's conditions met, Russia, the US, China, the G7, and all countries were finally on board. We managed to reach a consensus on the very first day of the Leaders' Summit, unlike at the 2022 Bali Summit, where negotiations on the declaration text dragged on until the final hours. This was no small feat. However, had we failed to achieve consensus, we had a well-prepared backup statement ready to highlight our dedication to global harmony. It would serve as an important reminder of our values and aspirations.

Reaching the Summit

Initially, we believed that the declaration would be announced the following day. However, following intense and complex negotiations, we thoroughly assessed the situation and reevaluated our stance. We decided to brief PM Modi, urging him to announce that very day instead of waiting.

He readily agreed—equally wanting to acknowledge the G20 consensus as soon as possible. Throughout the negotiations, he had been constantly enquiring about our progress and it was clear he understood the urgency of the moment. This strategic shift in timing added a layer of drama to the proceedings, as we recognized that in a situation full of uncertainty, it was crucial to seize the opportunity.

And so, after lunch on 9 September, PM Modi made the official announcement amid thunderous applause:

> *'Friends,*
>
> *We have just received good news. Due to the hard work of our teams and the support of all of you, the New Delhi G20 Leaders' Summit Declaration has been agreed on.*
>
> *I propose that we also adopt this Leaders' declaration. I declare to adopt this declaration. On this occasion, I would like to congratulate our Minister, Sherpa, and all the officials who have put in immense effort to make this worthwhile, and therefore, they all deserve to be congratulated.*[14]

His words carried the weight of collective effort and commitment, marking a milestone for all present. 'This declaration is not just an agreement; it's a shared vision for a balanced, equitable future.' He emphasized the necessity to 'move from "I" to "We" for sustainable solutions,' reminding us of our collective responsibility.

Following the PM's announcement, a press conference was convened where we proudly announced that India had successfully

---

[14]Haidar, Suhasini, 'G-20 Summit clinches New Delhi Declaration', *The Hindu*, 9 September 2023, https://tinyurl.com/mpd5uk73. Accessed on 9 September 2024.

secured consensus on all 83 paragraphs, all outcomes, and all documents, defying all odds.

As we broke the news, shockwaves rippled through the room. The journalists exchanged wide-eyed glances, their expressions shifting from disbelief to astonishment as they realized they would have to scramble to rewrite their stories on the fly. The prevailing sentiment was one of resignation; not a single person had anticipated success.

Amid the flashes of cameras and the buzz of journalists' questions, it became abundantly clear: India had not only risen to the occasion but had also rewritten the narrative before the eyes of the world. Without resorting to hyperbole, the G20 Summit's success in producing a consensus draft could be one of India's finest moments in multilateral diplomacy, coming especially when multilateralism and consensus-driven governance were on the wane.

One might ask if there were moments when we doubted our ability to reach this consensus. No doubt there were almost a dozen such moments, especially after the constant failures throughout the year. However, we remained resilient. Rather than succumbing to failures, we continually produced new drafts and maintained our creative, energetic and persistent approach.

Fears that China and Russia would not attend at the leaders' level on the day of the summit turned out to be somewhat of a blessing in disguise. Chinese President Xi Jinping's absence allowed the spotlight to remain firmly on the G20, and the declaration itself. This strategic move reinforced India's standing and underscored a significant victory for both India and the Global South. President Putin's absence was more than made up for by his later presence at the Virtual Summit.

We had made good on our promise to this 'One Earth, One Family, with One Future.'

For the Planet, People, Peace and Prosperity

In its ultimate form, the section on geopolitical issues in the NDLD expands on the discussion of the Ukraine conflict, dedicating an entire section of 8 paragraphs titled 'For the Planet, People, Peace and Prosperity.' It provides a detailed account of the adverse global impact of the conflict, touching upon issues like food and energy security, supply chains, macro-financial stability, inflation and growth. This expansion of details contributes to a more comprehensive understanding of the conflict's global implications.

The Bali paragraphs were split paragraphs, where the language reflected the divided views of members on a variety of issues. It records an 'agree to disagree' outcome, revealed in wording such as '*Most members strongly condemned the war in Ukraine* [...] *There were other views and different assessments of the situation and sanctions.*'[15] We realized the limitations of these divided perspectives, and pivoted our efforts to not only address the 'agree to disagree' outcomes seen in Bali, but to also foster a more cohesive and visionary approach toward addressing the complex geopolitical issues, particularly the Ukraine conflict. In this regard, the NDLD is wholly consensus-based, focusing on principles that the members collectively and unambiguously agree on.

While both declarations reference the conflict, the NDLD reinforces its commitment to international law by explicitly mentioning both the UN Security Council and UN General Assembly resolutions (A/RES/ES-11/1 and A/RES/ES-11/6). These resolutions underscore the importance of acting under the UN Charter's purposes and principles. This specificity strengthens the document's emphasis on the rule of law.

---

[15]G20 Bali Leaders' Declaration, Bali, Indonesia, 15–16 November 2022, The White House, https://tinyurl.com/yc3698eu. Accessed on 9 September 2024.

With External Affairs Minister Dr S. Jaishankar and Finance Minister Nirmala Sitharaman during the press briefing following the release of the New Delhi Leaders' Declaration.

External Affairs Minister Dr S. Jaishankar with his wife Kyoko Jaishankar aboard a cruise vessel on the Ganga in Varanasi during the Development Ministers' meeting.

The G20 logo, inspired by the vibrant colours of India's flag, featured Planet Earth cradled by the lotus, symbolizing growth amid challenges. Designed through an open competition on the MyGov portal, it embodied PM Modi's vision of *Jan Bhagidari*, reflecting active public participation during India's G20 presidency.

Padharo Mhare Desh: Delegates in vivid *saafas* enjoy a candid chat in Udaipur during the first G20 meeting of Sherpas.

Cultural diplomacy in action: G20 Sherpas experience vibrant Rajasthani tradition in Udaipur in December. They met turban master Pawan Vyas, who famously tied nearly half a kilometre of cloth in just 30 minutes.

G20 Sherpas enjoy a selfie moment in colourful saafas at Udaipur.

The iconic Taj Mahal Hotel in Mumbai is lit up in the tricolour during the first Development Working Group meeting in the city in December.

The stunning City Palace at Manek Chowk in Udaipur is lit up to mark the first G20 meeting of Sherpas under India's presidency.

A moment of hearty consensus at the second Sherpa meeting in Kumarakom, Kerala, in March.

A 'jumbo' experience: Delegates feed elephants at the Pobitora Wildlife Sanctuary in Assam in February, deepening their connection with these magnificent creatures.

Delegates take a scenic coracle ride on the Tungabhadra river in Hampi, Karnataka.

Culture Unites All: Lambani women artisans pose for a photo after entering the Guinness World Records for the 'Largest Display of Lambani Items' with 1,755 pieces, in Hampi. This initiative was supported by India's G20 Culture Working Group and led by the Ministry of Culture.

The immersive zone of the Culture Corridor at Bharat Mandapam showcased the intangible cultural heritage of India including Yoga, Vedic chanting, and the Kumbh Mela.

Atithi Devo Bhava: A delegate receives a warm welcome from Lakshmi, the temple elephant, outside the Virupaksha Temple in Hampi ahead of the third meeting of G20 Sherpas in July.

Traditional welcome in God's Own Country: Posing with delegates and Sherpas dressed in the traditional cotton mundus of Kerala.

G20 delegates capture a selfie at the Aga Khan Palace in Pune during the Education Working Group meeting in June.

Meeting French President Emmanuel Macron during the Summit.

Further, the New Delhi Declaration goes beyond rhetoric by calling for specific actions, like the full and timely implementation of agreements like the Black Sea Initiative related to grains, foodstuffs and fertilizers. It contextualizes these asks in terms of their disproportionate impact on developing and least-developed countries, particularly those in Africa, reinforcing the Declaration's spotlight on the often-overlooked needs of the Global South. It also underlines the importance of safeguarding peace and stability and working towards a comprehensive, just and durable peace in Ukraine. This collective stance ensures that the declaration is not merely symbolic but represents a commitment to addressing the real-world consequences of the conflict.

The impact of the geopolitical paragraphs in the NDLD continues to be felt by the international community. At the Berlin Global Dialogue in September 2023, all students, political thinkers, policy specialists, and members of government from the G7 to Russia were appreciative of India's ambitious efforts to drive consensus on development during such polarizing times. India has achieved consensus where even the United Nations Security Council (UNSC) and the G7 couldn't, and this would prove to be our lasting legacy in the highly charged multilateral arena.

On 10 September—the final day of India's G20 presidency—PM Modi welcomed world leaders to Rajghat, home to the eternal flame honouring Mahatma Gandhi. The atmosphere here said it all: we needed a powerful setting to cement our commitment to peace and non-violence, especially since tensions from the Russia-Ukraine conflict lingered over our discussions. All the leaders paused for a moment of silence, reflecting on Gandhi's enduring message of peace. With their heads bowed in tribute, leaders of the 21st century promised to work toward a world that knew peace.

Ultimately, India's adept handling of sensitive issues during the G20 transformed Rajghat into more than just a backdrop; it became a powerful symbol of reconciliation and our collective vision for a harmonious world.

This message of unity was reinforced when the leaders led by PM Modi came together for a ceremonial family photograph—a G20 tradition that reveals the dynamics between them. Barefoot leaders like German chancellor Olaf Scholz and Canadian PM Justin Trudeau navigated the wet ground, while President Biden and Brazil's President Luiz Inácio Lula da Silva opted for slippers.

Choosing Rajghat as our venue was especially meaningful—not only to honour Mahatma Gandhi but also to create a space where nations could come together with a shared commitment to the environment. The leaders' participation in a tree-planting initiative symbolized a unified pledge to environmental stewardship; it was about fostering a collective mindset centred on sustainability and our shared responsibility toward the Earth.

This was undoubtedly an ambitious endeavour that involved sourcing carefully selected saplings from G20 member countries that could thrive in India's varied climate. They were flown in from around the world. Once planted, these saplings would later be transplanted to the Bharat Mandapam, ensuring their continued growth and establishing a lasting green legacy in the heart of the city.

As these trees flourish over the years, they will serve as living reminders of a new way of thinking about our relationship with the planet—an ideological shift ignited by India's G20 presidency.

SIX

PIONEERING PROGRESS: LEADING THE GLOBAL SOUTH'S DIGITAL TRANSFORMATION

The shift from the analogue innovations of the Third Industrial Revolution to the dawn of digital electronics has fuelled unprecedented economic growth across the globe. At the turn of the 21st century, the computer became the poster child of this transformation, signalling the end of Industry 3.0 and the beginning of a new era. While the digital age is undeniably exciting, it has also magnified inequalities among people from varying socio-economic backgrounds. Digital technology has reshaped markets and our daily lives by revolutionizing industries, boosting production, research and development (R&D) capabilities, and streamlining supply chains. However, in tandem, income and wealth disparities within economies have risen steeply. Access to this technological revolution is often contingent upon reliable internet connectivity and the affordability of smartphones, leaving many behind.

The future of digitalization hinges on the effective capture, storage and exchange of, and access to, high-quality data. Many countries are leveraging such data to speed up their progress towards realizing the SDGs through innovative mechanisms. High-quality data allows countries to harness technological advances in research, invention, manufacturing, service delivery and finance. Verified data also provides individuals with digital identities, fostering greater participation in the digital economy. These digital identities hold promise for driving financial inclusion at reduced costs, offering access to savings, credit and welfare services. However, with these advancements come valid concerns over the safety of sensitive data and privacy.

Recognizing the transformative power of data in our lives, India has taken substantial steps to ensure data ownership and privacy for its citizens. With the Data Empowerment and Protection Architecture (DEPA) and the enactment of laws such as the Digital Personal Data Protection Act 2023 and the forthcoming Digital India Bill, India is delivering on this promise.

Our Constitution guarantees the right to privacy and empowers individuals to make autonomous choices. Embracing a human-centric approach, India has made significant strides in providing digital identity, affordable internet and bank accounts to billions. This vision culminated in creating the India Stack—a comprehensive set of digital public infrastructure that operates like a set of digital highways for countless private applications and services, empowering individuals and businesses alike. India Stack facilitates customer verification, market access and digital payments, and offers open credit and savings opportunities to billions of people.

In India, while individuals are the owners of their data, the government acts as the custodian, bearing the responsibility of keeping it secure. The increasing capabilities and prevalence of cybercrime exacerbate concerns about data privacy and protection. Robust cybersecurity measures are crucial for protecting our digital infrastructure, especially when personal data is involved. These measures do more than just safeguard information, they bolster confidence in the digital economy both for industry and individuals.

Yet, bridging the digital divide remains a challenge. Many factors contribute to this gap, from the unaffordability of internet access and smartphones to the lack of digital identities, bank accounts and cybersecurity. These hurdles hamper people's participation in the digital economy, stifling growth and development.

Digital exclusion is a significant impediment to socio-economic development. While the global internet penetration rate averages 67 per cent, it drops dramatically to 37 per cent in Africa.[1] The disparity is even starker when comparing high-income countries—where over 90 per cent of the population

[1]'Global offline population steadily declines to 2.6 billion people in 2023', Facts and Figures, 2023, International Telecommunication Union (ITU), https://tinyurl.com/e2kk9bpp. Accessed on 11 September 2024.

used the internet in 2022—to low-income countries, where only one in four individuals has internet access.[2] Globally, 850 million people lack any form of identification, with an estimated 470 million of them in sub-Saharan Africa.[3]

The advent of internet connectivity, data, cybersecurity and frontier technologies marks the cusp of the Fourth Industrial Revolution. Industry 4.0 brings with it the immense potential of the internet of things (IoT), machine learning (ML), the metaverse, and artificial intelligence (AI), particularly generative AI, to accelerate growth and development on a grand scale. Deep tech—melding cutting-edge science and technology in both hardware and software—is driving this new wave of innovation, poised to transform manufacturing, healthcare, clean energy and the digital economy in general.

However, the rapid and widespread adoption of frontier technologies may amplify the 'digital divide' into a 'technology divide', widening inequalities across the speed, scale and depth of technological changes. This divide threatens to increase disparities across regions, countries and communities, impacting jobs and livelihoods. Emerging markets may benefit from digitalization's economic growth and development, but low-income countries risk being left behind in the technological dust in the coming decades.

India's Digitalization Story: National Triumph, Global Acclaim

Ensuring the welfare and prosperity of 1.4 billion people from diverse backgrounds and regions requires inclusive and exhaustive

---

[2]Ibid.

[3]Clark, Julia, Anna Metz, and Claire Casher, '850 million people globally don't have ID—why this matters and what we can do about it', *World Bank Blogs*, 6 February 2023, https://tinyurl.com/4xvntu8y. Accessed on 24 September 2024.

plans for socio-economic development and growth. India's philosophy and commitment have been to take development to every citizen of India. PM Modi took this ethos from the grassroots implementation in India to the negotiation tables of the G20. To deliver on this mandate, we were tasked with ingraining inclusivity as our ethos across all G20 priorities and outcomes.

To prepare for this, we leaned on the rich experience embedded in India's governance archives, a nation daunting yet inspiring to govern. Having dedicated my entire career to contributing to the story of India—a story I deeply believed in, and which was strengthened through my experiences working with local fishermen in Kerala, who embraced change for the benefit of their communities, and leading the Aspirational Districts Programme (ADP) at NITI Aayog, where we saw the rise of the most backward districts of the country through smart, strategic community involvement. I understood early on that true change is driven by those who believe it is possible.

Thinking back over the last decade, India's story of digital transformation and financial inclusion emerged as a national triumph with the potential to change the world. We're not the first nation to embark on such a journey, but we're certainly the first developing country, with a relatively modest GDP per capita at 2,085.1[4] and 8,379.1.[5] Our ambition to create an accessible and affordable digital economy for all has helped us bridge divides across lines of geography, gender and income.

In 2009, India took its first bold step with the Aadhaar project, enrolling about 1.4 billion residents and covering nearly the entire adult population by 2023.[6] Aadhaar revolutionized the

[4]GDP per capita (constant 2015 US$)

[5]GDP per capita, PPP (current international $)

[6]'Approximately 99 pc adult population has been enrolled in Aadhaar: UIDAI CEO', *Unique Identification Authority of India*, https://tinyurl.com/dyr4twny.

way our government delivered services and subsidies. What's even more striking is how the private sector, especially in telecom and finance, leveraged Aadhaar for customer verification, slashing fraud, and expediting customer onboarding. This was the dawn of financial inclusion and digital transformation in India, now reaping benefits for our economy.[7]

Early in my career, working with traditional fishing communities in Kerala, I saw firsthand the nightmare of trying to open bank accounts for fishermen—a process that could take up to ten painful months under the weight of stringent know your customer (KYC) norms. This all began to change in 2014 when PM Modi introduced the Pradhan Mantri Jan-Dhan Yojana (PMJDY). This initiative aimed to make financial services readily accessible to everyone, including banking, remittances, credit, insurance and pensions. By 2023, the scheme had facilitated the opening of nearly 51.04 crore bank accounts.[8] The integration of Aadhaar with government registries formed a hub of welfare benefits centralized in a single Aadhaar-linked bank account. Tools like e-KYC, e-Sign, UPI, and Account Aggregator have enabled the Indian government, businesses, startups and developers to deliver financial services to our citizens. Coupled with PMJDY and mobile technology, Aadhaar democratized financial access, breathing vitality into our economy.

The World Bank noted an astounding reduction in customer acquisition and onboarding costs for Indian banks due to

---

Accessed on 11 September 2024.

[7]Gupta, Arvind, and Philip E. Auerswald, 'The Ups and Downs of India's Digital Transformation', *Harvard Business Review*, 6 May 2019, https://tinyurl.com/yrb7u3w4. Accessed on 11 September 2024.

[8]'51.04 crore Pradhan Mantri Jan Dhan Yojana (PMJDY) accounts opened with deposit balance of Rs. 2,08,855 crore', Ministry of Finance, 12 December 2023, https://tinyurl.com/4je7nrax. Accessed on 11 September 2024.

Aadhaar—from $23 to mere cents.[9] Between 2014 and 2017, over half of the new bank accounts worldwide were opened in India. By 2024, this number soared to 520 million, with these accounts totalling $27 billion, showcasing India's monumental progress towards financial inclusion.[10,11]

India was previously home to the world's largest unbanked population. Economists assumed this would persist for years to come. According to the Bank of International Settlements (BIS), India was not projected to reach a financial inclusion rate of 80 per cent until 2064. Things moved faster than expected. Almost 50 years faster, India met its financial inclusion goal by 2017, a level of progress in seven years for what would have taken 46 years.[12]

How did India pack half a century of progress into less than a decade? Our experience underscores the power of effective, inclusive DPIs that meet specific needs like identity, digital payments and trusted data exchange. When these elements come together, they form a potent stack of integrated applications that drastically shorten the developmental learning and adoption curve. This digital stack fosters innovation, supports open markets, and prevents monopolies while ensuring security, privacy and good

---

[9]World Bank, *G20 Policy Recommendations for Advancing Financial Inclusion and Productivity Gains through Digital Public Infrastructure*, Global Partnership for Financial Inclusion, 2023, https://tinyurl.com/y7wwhpcx. Accessed on 11 September 2024.

[10]PIB, '52.81 crore PM Jan-Dhan accounts with deposit balance of Rs. 2,30,792 crore opened as on 19.07.2024 under PMJDY', Ministry of Finance, https://tinyurl.com/3m5zp8vt. Accessed on 24 September 2024.

[11]Demirgüç-Kunt, Asli, et al., *The Global Findex Database 2017: Measuring Financial Inclusion and the Fintech Revolution*, https://tinyurl.com/4x7fy3e4. Accessed on 24 September 2024.

[12]D'Silva, Derryl, et al., *The design of digital financial infrastructure: lessons from India,* BIS Papers, No. 106, December 2019, https://tinyurl.com/yc6u9b6v. Accessed on 24 September 2024.

governance. As the World Bank has noted, DPIs can speed up economic development in low- or middle-income countries by at least a decade—and India stands as a shining example of this potential.

Our approach included both data protection and data empowerment. Based on this vision, NITI Aayog, in partnership with iSPIRT, developed a data governance policy framework, empowering Indians to control their data and use their digital history to access new growth opportunities.

This effort led to the creation of DEPA, a groundbreaking initiative that reimagines the conventional Western model. Instead of merely using data for advertising and sales, DEPA aims to empower one billion Indians. It introduces a robust techno-legal framework for data collaboration, be it public or personal data realms. At its heart lies a fundamental principle: data belongs to citizens, not service providers. This approach is crucial for non-personal public data, where the current regulatory framework fears the risk of de-anonymisation. DEPA guarantees that models train rather than memorize data, paving the way for responsible data sharing that fosters collaboration while ensuring privacy.

This extensive drive, fuelled by the DPI, significantly helped facilitate Direct Benefit Transfers (DBT), effectively reducing public expenditure leakages. The true value of DPI became apparent during the COVID-19 pandemic and subsequent lockdowns. Thanks to DPI, the government could transfer benefits directly to the bank accounts of 87 per cent of poor households within the initial months of the pandemic. Continuing to capitalize on this technology, the government transferred $83 billion (INR 6.9 lakh crore) under various schemes via DBT in FY 2024.[13]

In 2020, introducing an offline e-KYC service transformed

[13]Direct Benefit Transfer, Government of India, https://tinyurl.com/3bnjbv9x. Accessed on 24 September 2024.

identity verification in India. This digital innovation decimated the costs and complexity of traditional, paper-based KYC methods, essential for services like opening bank accounts and obtaining licenses. The adoption of Aadhaar's e-KYC soared from 30 million in 2015 to over 20 billion by 2024, showcasing the efficiency and user-friendliness of the digital verification system.[14]

The launch of the Unified Payments Interface (UPI) in 2016, enabling secure and fast payments between bank accounts, became a crucial building block of India Stack. Scaling UPI was a challenging task, and PM Modi was entrusted with creating a mass movement for digital payments in India by uniting government, banks and startups. Our team at NITI Aayog organized 100 'DigiDhan Melas' in 100 days, setting the momentum for today's digital payments landscape. UPI revolutionized digital payments, with 6.8 billion transactions recorded in September 2022 alone, facilitating seamless peer-to-peer transactions and significantly reducing cash reliance.[15]

The private sector also played a pivotal role in making the digital economy accessible to all. In 2016, Reliance Jio, a 4G-only network operator, revolutionized high-speed internet access across the nation by slashing mobile data costs by 96 per cent.[16] This boosted internet usage in the country, led to increased smartphone manufacturing, expanded internet access, and created digital identities and bank accounts, paving the way for secure digital payments.

---

[14]Unique Identification Authority of India, https://tinyurl.com/3t8bt6ab. Accessed on 24 September 2024.

[15]National Payments Corporation of India (NPCI) Monthly Metrics, https://tinyurl.com/byrtfvn4. Accessed on 24 September 2024.

[16]Khanna, Tarun, Anjali Raina, and Rachna Chawla, 'India Stack: Digital Public Infrastructure for All', Harvard Business School Case 724-371, July 2023 (Revised May 2024), https://tinyurl.com/akxrk9y3. Accessed on 24 September 2024.

Innovation that Leaves No One Behind

With a youthful population—an average age of 28—India's DPIs are set to capture the demographic dividend, democratizing technology for nearly 1.5 billion people. DPI revolutionizes how nations tackle complex societal problems, requiring innovative collaboration between the public and private sectors. It empowers countries to fast-track inclusive and competitive economic development by harnessing cutting-edge technology, good governance and market dynamics to achieve critical outcomes—in health, education, financial inclusion, human development, job creation and improved public services. Simply put, without DPI, speeding up the implementation of the SDGs would be nearly impossible.

For India, digital infrastructure has been a game changer, catapulting the startup ecosystem from around 350 startups in 2016 to over 120,000, including more than 120 unicorns by 2022.[17] Today, an Indian citizen can open a bank account, make a digital payment, get credit, buy insurance, and access social security benefits in less than a minute—all through a smartphone. The integration of UPI with fintech innovations like PhonePe, Google Pay and Paytm has accelerated this digital shift. Remarkably, digital transactions through UPI soared from just 91 crore in FY 2017 to 13,000 crore in FY 2023–24, accounting for 46 per cent of the world's digital.[18]

The impact of DPI extends far beyond payments, transforming the lending and insurance sectors as well. India has long faced a challenge known as the 'missing middle' in credit availability.

---

[17]Invest India, 'The Indian Unicorn Landscape', https://tinyurl.com/bdfzeywz. Accessed on 24 September 2024.

[18]'Growth of Various Modes of Digital Payments', https://tinyurl.com/4fkj85pk. Accessed on 24 September 2024.

Large companies were able to secure loans easily, and microfinance institutions catered to very small businesses. However, MSMEs were caught in a gap, struggling with a credit shortfall.

Then came the Open Credit Enablement Network (OCEN), transforming the lending landscape. It shifted the focus from asset-based lending to a more flexible, cash-flow-based model, using factors like income and tax returns. This approach opened credit access for small business owners, who previously relied on personal savings or high-interest informal lenders.

Fintech startups like MobiKwik, BillDesk, Razorpay, BharatPe and Zerodha disrupted traditional models. Zerodha transformed stock trading with its efficient platform, while Cred redefined credit card bill payments and rewards. Digital lending platforms like Lendingkart, KreditBee and MoneyTap addressed the credit needs of underserved markets, advancing financial inclusion. The Account Aggregator (AA) network further transformed lending by enabling secure, consent-based sharing of financial records.

This transformation, boosted by accessible credit through OCEN and seamless UPI transactions, aligns with India's push for local economic growth. It is laying the groundwork for a more inclusive and thriving economy.

India's proactive approach has created opportunities for grassroots empowerment, with artificial intelligence (AI) as the next frontier. The World Economic Forum estimates that AI could add $1 trillion to India's economy by 2035.[19] AI's potential spans clean air, health, education and governance. Initiatives like Jugalbandi and Bhashini break language barriers, improving access to services and information. In healthcare, innovators leveraging AI like Dozee are revolutionizing patient

[19]Nair, Mohit, and Arathi Sethumadhavan, 'AI in healthcare: India's trillion-dollar opportunity', *World Economic Forum*, https://tinyurl.com/yuh6hz5x. Accessed on 24 September 2024.

monitoring. The banking sector is also benefiting, with AI enhancing customer experiences and boosting operational efficiency, projecting significant savings.

India's AI strategy emphasizes openness, transparency and collaboration, fostering partnerships and promoting global standards. The IndiaAI Mission aims to drive AI innovation through public-private partnerships (PPP) and support deep-tech startups, catalyzing research and development.

From 2015 to 2023, India has showcased remarkable growth in AI skills, leading the world in this expansion. The Stanford AI Index Report highlights India's leading position in AI skills growth.[20] In 2023 alone, AI talent hiring grew by 16.8 per cent, reflecting the emphasis on AI capabilities. This trend spans various industries, not just technology.

Globally, India has the second-highest number of GitHub AI projects. This engagement shows the country's active role in AI development. Projects like UdyogYantra assess the nutritional quality of midday meals in Gadchiroli, and the PM KISAN chatbot aids farmers, demonstrating how AI impacts grassroots.

India's vibrant startup scene, with AI-centric ventures like Sarvam AI, is building AI tools in Indian languages and making their tools open-source. Digital Green has helped farmers in multiple languages to navigate climate change, implement best practices, and bring their crops to market. These startups leverage AI for societal good, positioning India to lead in the AI era. For the Global South, with fewer legacy systems, this digital wave is perfectly poised for transformative change.

[20]Maslej, Nestor, et al., 'The AI Index Report 2024', AI Index Steering Committee, Institute for Human-Centered AI, Stanford University, April 2024, https://tinyurl.com/4ew4tja2. Accessed on 24 September 2024.

From Smartphones to Negotiation Tables

As Sherpa, I had the opportunity to witness the emergence of a new chapter in global development through digitalization.

India has consistently been ahead of the curve in leveraging digital technology for economic growth. Our journey is driven by a blend of inclusion and innovation, creating a digital economy that reaches everyone and is powered by everyone. Both startups and tech giants like Google are using DPI to offer groundbreaking services. Improved data capture, storage and exchange capabilities enable us to bring individuals onto a single digital platform, propelling us into Industry 4.0. To me, DPI offers a blueprint for cost-effective, secure and last-mile digital solutions that both protect and empower citizens.

Without similar capabilities, Global South countries risk falling behind, widening the technology divide. India has inspired several countries to pursue inclusive, safe and equitable digital systems. Through the India Stack Global Initiative, we have signed memorandums of understanding (MoUs) with nations like Armenia, Sierra Leone, Suriname, and Antigua and Barbuda. Many others are also in discussions, seeking India's expertise in implementing DPI.

Serving as India's G20 Sherpa allowed me to advance India's vision of human-centric development through DPI from a national success to a globally recognized framework. The journey was intricate and fascinating, marked by pivotal moments at the G20 Summit that highlighted DPI's growing importance.

India's experience with DPI, particularly India Stack, is a story worth telling. Our transformation from a nation struggling with financial exclusion to a model of digital inclusivity is inspiring. UPI caught the attention of the world with its real-time transaction capability across diverse banking platforms, showcasing seamless consumer behaviour and financial inclusion.

In conversations with international delegates, we often shared UPI's transformative tales, sparking deeper discussions about replicating such systems globally. The G20 Secretariat organized notable events featuring influential leaders such as Nick Clegg, President of Global Affairs at Meta, whose strategic insights into digital governance were invaluable. Philanthropist Bill Gates brought his deep expertise and philanthropic vision, consistently advocating for technology that drives social progress. Queen Máxima of the Netherlands, a passionate advocate for DPI, demonstrated her tremendous knowledge and fervour in promoting digital transformation. The Chairman and CEO of Microsoft, Satya Nadella, and its President, Brad Smith, highlighted the importance of leveraging technology for sustainable growth, emphasizing the critical role of collaboration between the public and private sectors. Prof. Jeffrey Sachs emphasized the significance and importance of DPI in achieving SDGs.

These forums highlighted DPI's societal benefits and showcased how it could align with diverse business models and interests, despite being distinct from Western digital infrastructure models.

The Global DPI Summit and related events organized in Pune, Maharashtra, in June 2023 demonstrated DPI's versatility across various sectors. Real breakthroughs came during meetings with private sector leaders led by the Ministry of Electronics and Information Technology (MeitY). These interactions were diplomatic and persuasive efforts to navigate apprehensions and showcase DPI as a global digital game changer.

Our collaboration with the United Nations Development Programme (UNDP), particularly under its administrator Achim Steiner, helped spread the narrative around DPI. These interactions were vital for articulating how DPI could enhance development efforts across the Global South. The toolkits UNDP is developing to help implement DPI in various countries are significant steps towards wider digital inclusion. Furthermore, the G20's push for DPI has aligned well with the UN's High Impact Initiative on DPI, aiming for digitalization in 100 countries by 2030—a goal that India actively supports.

Recognizing the power of DPI to tackle multifaceted problems, a G20 task force was created with the mission of guiding member countries in enhancing productivity and shaping digital economy policies. Co-chairing this task force with Nandan Nilekani, former Chairman of UIDAI, was a wonderful experience in technology diffusion. Our group included influential figures as well as key leaders from ministries overseeing finance, electronics, external affairs, and more. It was energizing to be surrounded by such minds, each bringing their unique perspectives and expertise to the table. Our collective efforts focused on drafting a comprehensive report that tackled the complexities of scaling DPI on a global level. In our report, we explained the DPI approach using India's example and provided a strategic blueprint to scale DPI across sectors and globally.

Our report highlights the transformative role of DPI in driving economic transformation, financial inclusion, and development. It outlines how DPI, through digital identity systems, interoperable payments, and consent-based data sharing, has revolutionized public service delivery in India, lifting millions out of poverty and enabling access to education, healthcare and financial services. India's DPI, exemplified by initiatives like Aadhaar, UPI, and the Data Empowerment and Protection Architecture (DEPA), is credited with significantly enhancing transparency, efficiency and inclusion. The report emphasizes the global relevance of DPI, noting that it allows nations to leapfrog traditional development stages by fostering innovation, reducing transaction costs, and maintaining competition through open, interoperable systems.

International organizations, including the World Bank, have endorsed DPI as a powerful tool for advancing financial inclusion and productivity gains. A report by the G20 Finance Track, developed in partnership with the World Bank, underscores how DPI can bridge gaps in the financial sector, reduce transaction costs, and stimulate market competition. The UNDP and the International Monetary Fund (IMF) have also highlighted DPI's potential to accelerate progress towards the Sustainable Development Goals (SDGs) and enhance public service delivery, particularly in low- and middle-income countries. DPI has gained global acceptance, with multilateral bodies such as the EU and the US recognizing its value in fostering open and inclusive digital economies. In those moments, we realized how vital our work could be in reshaping economies and elevating public services through digital advancements. The report we produced was not just a set of policy recommendations, but also a strategic blueprint that could guide countries in developing their digital infrastructures to transform the way they deliver public services and build trust with their citizens.

As our discussions deepened, we witnessed a significant shift in how DPI was perceived amongst G20 members. I distinctly remember the debates around the term itself. Initially, we grappled with calling it 'digital public goods (DPG)', but gradually we realized that 'digital public infrastructure' better described our vision. This evolution wasn't merely semantic but also illustrated our growing understanding and consensus on the importance of a strong digital foundation for all nations. This transformation was largely due to the relentless efforts of then Secretary Alkesh Kumar Sharma and Sushil Pal, Joint Secretary of MeitY, who engaged in thoughtful consultations with various delegations and showcased the true value of DPI.

The bilateral negotiations were particularly complex, especially with representatives from China and the US. Both countries, with their advanced technological ecosystems, viewed DPI with a mix of curiosity and caution, as it could disrupt their existing digital economies. I recall discussing how these nations could maintain their autonomy while collaborating to build and manage DPI. The conversations were challenging, yet essential, and each exhibition showcasing DPI use cases played a pivotal role in breaking down barriers and reaching consensus.

As negotiations around DPI and digitalization advanced, the richer and more nuanced the conversations became. Our discussions went beyond technology itself; we envisioned a future where digital infrastructure could serve as a unifying force for global development.

I particularly remember a meeting we held with the secretaries of the various ministries managing the G20 WGs. We gathered to align India's priorities for the summit, particularly the rapid digitalization of sectors like agri-tech, health, tourism and trade through DPI. It was here that we confronted the realities of increasing digitalization—the risks and challenges it brought, along with the urgent need to upskill our workforce. This meeting helped craft a vision for comprehensive multi-sectoral digital solutions that could genuinely transform lives across the globe.

In agri-tech, we explored how DPI could revolutionize the agricultural landscape. We saw firsthand how Indian startups were already making impressive strides in this area. They were using DPI to connect farmers directly to markets, ensuring they received fair prices for their produce while simultaneously reducing waste. This model, we believed, could be replicated in other countries, empowering farmers and strengthening food security.

The health sector's transformation through DPI was equally interesting. We envisioned a future where health data could be shared seamlessly across platforms, enhancing patient care and driving cutting-edge medical research. This vision was already turning into reality in India, and we were eager to share our lessons with the world.

The trade sector was also witnessing a transformation as digital platforms allowed small businesses to reach global markets. This fostered sustainable tourism and inclusive trade practices. These sectors, which are so important for the economies of the Global South, could be rejuvenated by DPI creating opportunities for many.

Various WGs achieved significant outcomes on DPI. These efforts showcased the cross-cutting nature of our solutions and paved the way for the universal adoption of DPI.

The Global Partnership for Financial Inclusion (GPFI), in collaboration with the World Bank, shared a comprehensive report entitled 'G20 Policy Recommendations for Advancing Financial Inclusion & Productivity Gains through Digital Public Infrastructure.'[21] This report was endorsed by G20 Finance Ministers, Central Bank Governors, and Leaders alike, offering actionable recommendations to improve financial inclusion and productivity through DPI. It highlighted how DPI could dramatically reduce transaction costs, encourage innovation, and bridge financial disparities, contributing to inclusive growth and sustainable development.

The Health Working Group launched the 'G20 Global Initiative on Digital Health' under the WHO, which focuses on digital health innovations. This initiative aimed to democratize health technology through open-source solutions and interoperability, creating a repository of digital healthcare solutions that would

---

[21]World Bank, *G20 Policy Recommendations for Advancing Financial Inclusion and Productivity Gains through Digital Public Infrastructure*, https://tinyurl.com/36euua2y. Accessed on 12 September 2024.

particularly benefit low- and middle-income countries.

The Agriculture Working Group focused on developing open-access agricultural platforms to enhance operational efficiency through sustainable practices. Their goal was to improve the quality of agricultural data and interoperability between databases, promoting innovation in agri-informatics.

The Trade and Investment Working Group crafted 'common principles' for the compilation of financial data for MSMEs, and 'guiding principles' aimed at reducing entry barriers for these businesses on digital platforms. They proposed developing a Meta Information Portal for MSMEs while establishing principles for the adoption of digital technologies in logistics. The Education Working Group worked to make tech-enabled learning more inclusive, qualitative and collaborative, sharing successful DPI applications and discussing innovative approaches to bridge the divide in education and skill development.

However, it was during the sessions of the Digital Economy Working Group that we reached a key milestone in our journey—the definition of DPI was collectively understood. It felt monumental to know that the G20 leaders backed this framework. It was gratifying to witness DPI as a vital and well-defined component of a renewed digital landscape—one that ensures secure identity, facilitates fast payments, and enables seamless data sharing.

All these discussions underscored how transformative DPI could be in the lives of citizens and in addressing global crises, evolving from merely theoretical discussions to a concept that found its way into the NDLD:

> 'Technology can enable rapid transformations for bridging the existing digital divides and accelerate progress for inclusive and sustainable development. Digital public infrastructure (DPI), as an evolving concept and as a set of shared digital systems, built and leveraged by both the

> public and private sectors, based on secure and resilient infrastructure, and built on open standards and specifications, as well as open-source software, can enable the delivery of services at a societal scale.'

When there is a clear consensus on concepts like DPI, it creates a bedrock for coherent policy formulation and facilitates smoother cross-border knowledge sharing. With a shared understanding, countries can align their strategies effectively, paving the way for meaningful collaboration.

The inclusion of DPI in the NDLD was not a fleeting mention, but was interwoven in various chapters and the preamble. This strategic placement highlighted DPI's role as a multi-sector solution, showcasing its versatility and broad applications in areas such as financial inclusion, healthcare and education.

▪

As the rise of generative AI in 2022 coincides with our presidency, we were determined to include a paragraph in the NDLD addressing the significance of AI. Initially, AI was absent from the notes circulated among the participating countries. However, we felt the G20 leaders needed to commit the world's leading economies to utilize AI responsibly and for the benefit of all.

We collaborated with leading experts to draft the paragraphs on AI that would guide global cooperation, while also being mindful of potential risks. These comprehensive drafts had to outline India's perspective on AI regulation, innovation and governance, striking a balance among all three.

I met Sam Altman, the co-founder and CEO of OpenAI, during his visit to India in June 2023. Our brief interaction offered valuable insights into his perspective on AI, particularly generative AI, which represents the aspirations of emerging entrepreneurs in the space. Sam expressed that while AI could catalyze unprecedented wealth and prosperity, it also posed risks that could exacerbate societal conflicts. He highlighted the importance of international regulation to mitigate these risks and suggested that an oversight body similar to the International Atomic Energy Agency (IAEA) be established for AI.

The National Association of Software and Service Companies (NASSCOM) published a set of guidelines designed to establish a framework for generative AI. Our draft emphasized a pro-innovation approach to governance and stressed the role of AI in fostering sustainable development. As the Voice of the Global South, the document underscored the importance of equitably sharing the benefits of AI while addressing its risks.

The first draft resonated powerfully with G20 members, many of whom were still planning their approaches to generative AI—a topic that had only recently entered mainstream conversation. There was a palpable sense that we should continue to adopt a pro-innovation stance, and several nations argued it was too early to impose regulations.

During our virtual negotiations, the paragraph was gaining traction—all G20 countries eventually adopted it. To our surprise, finalizing the language took much less time than we had expected. By the end of our discussions, the G20 presented a proactive stance on AI, offering much-needed direction in a rapidly evolving digital landscape. This move aligned India's digital economy with the wider goals of the G20, positioning us as a role model for the world to emulate.

India has been keen to future-proof its progress in the digital economy from the outset, and integrating AI with DPI seemed a natural step forward. The synergy between the two could amplify efficiency in service delivery, create inclusive systems catering to diverse populations, and improve both monitoring capabilities and predictive analytics. The AI4Bharat models illustrated how open-source AI initiatives could significantly enhance digital inclusivity and language accessibility.[22] A new era of computing and automation began with the advancement of machine learning techniques and the utilization of massive datasets. With foundational models serving as DPI, startups could access a more relevant set of AI-powered products, allowing citizens and national companies to tailor models to their specific use cases.

India's balanced approach to AI regulation aims to do more than simply enforce rules; it nurtures innovation within a secure framework. It grants opportunities to develop local AI models built on indigenous datasets, liberating nations from the risks of monopolization. India wants to nurture an AI ecosystem that not only prevents monopolies and ethical biases but also safeguards privacy. This vision encourages the creation of AI solutions that are tailored to the local context, while also possessing the potential for global applicability.

Techade for Global South

For the Global South, DPI is far more than just a technological upgrade; it represents a leap towards inclusive and sustainable development tailored to the unique needs and circumstances of each nation. It is therefore no surprise that under India's stewardship, the outcomes related to DPI at the G20 Summit marked a substantial leap towards a digitally inclusive future.

As the G20 concluded, the leaders gathered virtually under the leadership of PM Modi, announcing significant outcomes related to DPI. The establishment of a Social Impact Fund (SIF), for which India had pledged $25 million, symbolized our commitment to nurturing DPI on a global scale.

---

[22]AI4Bharat, a research lab at IIT Madras, is dedicated to advancing AI technology for Indian languages through open-source contributions.

The SIF is envisioned as a pivotal resource and catalyst for digital transformation, particularly in the Global South, which has felt the profound impacts of the pandemic and its aftermath. What sets the SIF apart is that it is not just about financial help—it is a comprehensive resource hub dedicated to developing and deploying DPI.

The fund will provide the necessary financial backing to nations working to develop DPIs, ensuring that monetary constraints do not impede their transformative journey. It aims to attract contributions from international players, including private sector participants, to help scale DPI efforts across countries. International contributions to the SIF will allow it to offer assistance tailored to the specific needs and priorities of individual countries. This approach ensures that countries can adopt and adapt DPI in a way that addresses poverty, combats inequality, and creates opportunities for all. The DPI framework allows nations to choose their starting point based on their priorities, their current digital preparedness, and resource availability.

Beyond just funding, the SIF will offer a wide range of technical and non-technical support, strengthening the capacities of countries to build robust digital infrastructures.

As DPI gains traction across diverse settings, national policymakers can draw on case studies to tackle specific development challenges. Collaboration will be vital, enabling best practices and lessons learned to be shared worldwide—an essential element for countries at different stages of DPI development.

The urgent establishment of the Global Digital Public Infrastructure Repository (GDPIR) within two months of the NDLD demonstrated the importance we attached to DPI. The GDPIR, which captures the essence and insights from our digital transformation, now boasts 54 DPIs from 16 countries. This repository was designed to facilitate the exchange of DPI knowledge and development, functioning as a central platform for sharing implementations from various governments. By addressing knowledge gaps in decision-making and implementation, the GDPIR aimed to assist nations in effectively designing, deploying and managing their DPIs.

India's leadership at the G20 also initiated the One Future Alliance (OFA), a voluntary initiative to build capacity and provide technical assistance and financial support for implementing DPI in low- and middle-income countries.

India envisioned its role in the global adoption of DPI not as a leader but as a mentor, sharing its expertise and technology through initiatives like the Modular Open-Source Identity Platform (MOSIP). Today, MOSIP has provided identity to more than 110 million residents across 17 countries.

The term 'Techade' embodies the vision of an inclusive and sustainable future driven by technological systems that leave no one behind. The foundations laid during India's G20 presidency are set to catalyze further innovations and forge new partnerships. As Brazil prepares to take the helm of the G20 presidency, the groundwork established by India's focus on DPI and AI offers a roadmap for swift, inclusive development. The journey ahead brims with possibilities and challenges, but the path we've charted stands clear. By ensuring that innovation remains accessible to all, we can create a world where technology is not a privilege reserved for the few, but a universal right.

Reflecting on the journey of DPI at the G20, I see a narrative rich in transformation, collaboration and foresight. India is paving the way for a Global South-led digital transformation in this century, where global cooperation lies at its core.

SEVEN

FROM VISION TO LEGACY

India's G20 presidency will be remembered as the most ambitious in recent years. Our presidency covered 73 lines of effort in the NDLD, twice as many as the Indonesian presidency in 2022. With nearly 40 documents annexed, which are presidency documents and do not include the WG outcome documents, this number was again almost double the average number of documents annexed.

TABLE 3

Country	Outcomes (Line of Effort)	Annexed Documents*	Total
India 2023	87	118	**205**
Indonesia 2022	27	23	**50**
Italy 2021	36	29	**65**
Saudi Arabia 2020	22	8	**30**
Japan 2019	13	16	**29**
Argentina 2018	12	21	**33**
Germany 2017	8	14	**22**

India more than delivered on our agenda. We delivered on issues of global importance, such as the SDGs, climate action, and growth. We delivered on technological transformation and women-led development. With 83 paragraphs, all agreed to by 100 per cent consensus, we matched ambition with action during our presidency.

We rewrote records and created lasting legacies, the most prominent being the inclusion of the African Union (AU) within the G20 fold.

'Modi's Guarantee': G20 becomes G21

As the New Delhi Leaders' Summit approached, the G20 Leaders' Declaration was poised to highlight India's progressive ideas and inclusive approach. Known as the 'Mother of Democracy', India had the additional weight of carrying a legacy that transcended conventional democratic timelines. This title reflects a democratic framework and heritage dating back to the Indus Valley Civilization and the Sangam period, where the first evidence of structured institutions and systems of governance emerged. Ancient texts like the *Rigveda* and *Arthashastra* introduce democratic practices in early India, emphasizing the importance of collective decision-making and public welfare.

India's democratic journey has seen the continuity and evolution of these ideals. From the princely states to a united republic, the commitment to democratic values and inclusive governance has been all-pervasive. As the world's largest democracy, India's G20 presidency had to reflect these principles, ensuring that all voices were heard.

Including the AU as a permanent member of the G20 became a torchbearer for this spirit, reinforcing the idea that the G20 is a global democratic meeting that ensures a significant alignment of interests between the Global North and South. This formal admission signified a transformative moment in global governance, marking a shift towards a more inclusive and representative international order where the voices of previously marginalized nations gained prominence.

The seeds of this significant diplomatic achievement were planted at the 2022 G20 Summit in Bali with a promise made between two world leaders. Senegalese President Macky Sall, the AU Chair, shared his frustration with PM Modi and Indonesian President Joko Widodo that there were no talks about AU membership at the G20. In response, PM Modi assured him that this matter would be addressed during India's presidency, affirming it as 'Modi's guarantee'. This commitment reflected a vision of inclusivity and reaffirmed India's dedication to amplifying Africa's voice on the global stage.

India has always been a dependable partner in Africa's developmental journey. Over the past ten years, India's engagement with Africa has blossomed. Trade between India and African nations surged to $98 billion in the fiscal year 2022–23, up from $89.6 billion in the previous year. India has extended over $12.37 billion in concessional loans to the continent, positioning itself as one of the top five investors in Africa.[1]

Despite the vast oceans separating us, a spirit rooted in independence and self-determination intertwined our fates. Both regions drew inspiration from each other's struggles for freedom, fostering a camaraderie that transcended geographical boundaries. The world bore witness to India and Africa finding their rightful place in the community of nations, their paths of common destiny continuing to intertwine. This deep-rooted belief became the foundation of India's foreign policy—an understanding that our progress remains incomplete without the development of Africa.

However, this view was not initially unanimous at the G20. There was a huge debate at the Sherpa level on whether the members of the AU should be granted full membership of the G20 or included as special invitees. Members also raised the issue of whether other regional bodies, such as ASEAN (Association of Southeast Asian Nations) and MERCOSUR (or the Southern Common Market), should be included. I found myself in the thick of these discussions, guiding the arguments and drawing critical distinctions. We argued that much like the EU, the AU

[1]Mattoo, Shashank, 'Confident that India-Africa trade will cross $100 billion: EAM Jaishankar', *Mint*, 14 June 2023, https://tinyurl.com/53zkj3eu. Accessed on 25 September 2024.

was a formal institution with a pan-African parliament, unlike ASEAN or MERCOSUR.

Believing strongly that if the EU had full membership, the AU deserved the same, we knew we needed more than just strong arguments. We relied heavily on PM Modi's credibility and influence. In June, the PM sent letters to all G20 leaders, advocating full membership for the AU. Thereafter, discussions increasingly focused on issues relevant to the Global South, and the presence of the AU became a natural fit.

At the Leaders' Summit, we planned a special session to commemorate the inclusion of AU into the G20. The President of the Union of the Comoros, Azali Assoumani, who was also the Chair of the AU, was seated next to Australia before the formal G20 deliberations. This symbolic gesture effectively gave the AU a genuine seat at the table. When President Assoumani hugged PM Modi amid applause, it was a powerful visual. The image made the front pages of newspapers worldwide, sending a clear signal of India's commitment to amplifying the voices of the Global South in global affairs.

As the G20 deliberations drew to a close, the AU's permanent membership became a historic reality, integrating 55 African nations into the forum and expanding its reach to 80 per cent of the world's population. This momentous achievement, which resonated far beyond Africa's borders, marked a victory for the principles of fairness, equity and balanced global representation. In a world marked by evolving geopolitical alliances and complex economic interests, this milestone heralded a new era of international cooperation and representation for the AU, India, and the entire world, with the potential to redefine global decision-making as we know it today.

This success was born from persistent advocacy and PM Modi's leadership, which brought the idea from the periphery of global discourse to the spotlight of diplomatic considerations during India's G20 presidency. This move reinforces the idea that every nation, regardless of its size or economic prowess, has a stake in shaping the future of the world. It also reflects the recognition of the AU as an essential ally in confronting global challenges while advancing shared goals of peace, prosperity and sustainable development.

The integration of the AU into the G20 also brings strategic advantages for India. It strengthens economic ties and opens new avenues for collaboration with African nations. Furthermore, it aligns perfectly with India's long-term foreign policy objectives, supporting our advocacy for multilateral reforms and a more inclusive G20.

Reflecting on this achievement, I think of each step—the meticulous planning, the intense negotiations, and the moments of uncertainty. The inclusion of the AU was a promise made and kept by PM Modi, reflecting the gratitude expressed by President Sall during the BRICS Summit in Johannesburg days before the G20 Summit in New Delhi. His appreciation highlighted the transformative impact of dedicated leadership.

Boost to *Nari Shakti*

In the pursuit of creating a more inclusive world, India has taken inspiring steps toward achieving gender parity. As a nation, we have implemented a series of proactive policies and programmes aimed at empowering women across various spheres. PM Modi's key initiatives such as the Women's Reservation Act 2023 reflect the commitment to tangible action. The Act, a landmark in India's legislative landscape, seeks to enhance women's representation in political spheres, ensuring their voices contribute significantly to decision-making processes.

Comparative analysis with other post-colonial countries highlights India's leading role in enacting crucial measures for gender equality. Beyond its borders, India's commitment to women's empowerment is evident in its robust support for international initiatives. The nation's contributions to UN Women, for instance, play a significant role in advancing gender equality globally.

Domestically, the recognition of 'Nari Shakti' (women power) highlighted the transformative potential of women in driving societal progress. This narrative took centre stage during the G20 presidency, illustrating the nation's commitment to placing women at the heart of development initiatives. The focus on women-led development reflected India's rich traditions, complemented by a forward-thinking approach to building a more inclusive and equitable society.

Instead of viewing women solely as recipients of opportunities, there was a fundamental shift towards recognizing their role as leaders and changemakers. This wasn't merely a rhetorical adjustment, but a call to action necessitating concrete policies that positioned women at the forefront of decision-making processes, thereby challenging and transforming existing systems. This was evident at the G20 tables, where discussions emphasized the need for women to lead the discourse and shape the socio-economic landscape. To create a world where women wield substantial influence, we recognized the importance of moving beyond inclusion to active participation.

India's G20 presidency embodied this paradigm shift. Gender equality, women's empowerment, and women-led development became the backbone of our policy considerations. We pursued historic efforts towards gender parity through platforms like EMPOWER led by Sangita Reddy, Joint Managing Director of Apollo Hospitals, W20 led by Dr Sandhya Purecha, Chairman of

Sangeet Natak Akademi, and the Ministerial on Empowerment of Women. EMPOWER provided a comprehensive platform to address challenges hindering women's progress and to create an environment where they could thrive personally and professionally. The W20 and the Ministerial on Empowerment of Women further solidified the G20's commitment to dismantling barriers, ensuring women were active leaders and decision-makers in global development.

These developments showed that our collective efforts needed to transcend female labour force participation. The focus was on a fundamental shift in perspective, ensuring women-led development agendas, and transforming the socio-economic fabric to be more empowering for all.

However, promoting women-led development faced significant challenges. Many countries insisted on UN terminology like 'gender equality' and argued against women-led development. Our push for women-led development met severe resistance, but through ambitious, aggressive, forward-looking negotiations, we saw women-led development through. The US acknowledged our progress, calling it the most ambitious draft ever seen in a multilateral forum. Special credit goes to Nagaraj, who led these critical discussions.

On the direction of PM Modi, our relentless efforts set the stage for a groundbreaking initiative, highlighting the significance of women-led development. The NDLD underscored the essential role of gender equality and female leadership, emphasizing how empowering women and girls could accelerate progress towards the 2030 Agenda.

India's comprehensive strategy rested on four key pillars:

- The first, 'Enhancing Economic and Social Empowerment', aimed to break down barriers hindering women's progress and ensure equal access to resources.

- The second, 'Bridging the Gender Digital Divide', focused on providing women with equitable opportunities in the digital world.
- 'Driving Gender-Inclusive Climate Action' recognized the unique challenges climate change poses for women and incorporated a gender-sensitive approach to climate initiatives.
- Last, 'Securing Women's Food Security, Nutrition, and Well-Being' addressed crucial aspects of women's health, emphasizing access to nutritious food and healthcare.

These pillars formed a multi-faceted approach, showcasing a holistic strategy for the global empowerment of women. By addressing economic, technological, environmental and health-related dimensions, India's G20 presidency aimed to create a supportive environment for the comprehensive development of women worldwide. This initiative showed a deep commitment to tackling the diverse challenges that women face, recognizing their essential role in achieving sustainable and inclusive development. The interconnected nature of these pillars was crucial, reflecting the complex realities of women's lives and the multifaceted approach needed to support them effectively.

Recognizing the multifaceted challenges women face, India's G20 presidency established a Working Group on Women's Empowerment. This significant initiative, driven by India and supported by the Troika countries, aims to address various challenges women encounter. The inaugural meeting of this working group was set for 2024, coinciding with Brazil's G20 presidency, marking a collective effort to advance women's empowerment globally. Alongside the Disaster Risk Resilience Working Group and the Startup20 Engagement Group, this initiative stands as a prominent legacy of India's impactful G20 presidency. It reflects India's leadership and PM Modi's commitment to advancing women's empowerment, contributing to a more inclusive and resilient future as reflected in our commitment to *Sabka Saath, Sabka Vikas, Sabka Vishwas, Sabka Prayas.*

IMEC: Redefining Trade Routes

Yet another prominent legacy is the India-Middle East-Europe Economic Corridor (IMEC), one of the most ambitious geoeconomic and geopolitical projects India has signed.

For centuries, the only way to reach Asia from Europe was to sail around the Cape of Good Hope. In 1498, Vasco da Gama charted an alternative sea route from Europe to India, which changed the face of maritime trade in Europe and Asia. A few hundred years later, much of the Indian subcontinent was colonized, and the UK controlled much of the trade originating from India. Their ships carried goods from India, sailing past the Cape of Good Hope, depositing and picking up cargo from various British warehouses along the way.

Competing European colonial powers, such as France, felt the need for a new route to Asia, which would connect the Mediterranean Sea to the Red Sea through a canal—the Suez Canal. With initial efforts led by France, there was vehement opposition from the UK against the project, as it would jeopardize its trade interests, particularly with India. However, just twenty years after the opening of the Suez Canal in 1869, the UK gained control of the canal during the Anglo-Egyptian War of 1882.

After World War II, Egyptian President Gamal Abdel Nasser nationalized the canal, leading to the Suez Crisis of 1956. This led to the creation of the United Nations Emergency Force (UNEF), mandated to maintain the peace at the borders of Egypt and Israel. India was one nation to contribute troops to this peacekeeping mission. Since then, there have been several more closures because of tensions between the Arab nations and Israel. Today, the Multinational Force and Observers (MFO) enforces the terms of the Egypt-Israel peace treaty of 1978.

In recent years, the Red Sea route to international trade has come under increasing stress. According to World Bank data, close to 30 per cent of the world's container traffic passes through the Red Sea.[2] First, we saw the Ever Given incident in 2021, in which the ship blocked the Suez Canal, disrupting the world's most critical shipping route for several days. This led to massive supply chain disruptions. In October 2023, war broke out between Israel and Hamas following devastating attacks on civilians. In retaliation, groups such as the Houthi in Yemen commenced attacks on ships bound for Israel in the Red Sea, disrupting global shipping. By March 2024, traffic through the Suez Canal had dropped by more than 50 per cent. Shipping companies took the long way around, with traffic through the Cape of Good Hope increasing by more than 100 per cent.[3] Not only are these longer routes raising costs and taking longer, but they are also burning more carbon.

There is a need for an alternative route that connects Europe and India, one that can compete with the Red Sea shipping routes in times of normalcy, and act as a buffer for supply chain disruptions in times of crisis. One such initiative was launched by China as part of the Belt and Road Initiative (BRI). It was launched in 2013 with the goal of an overland route connecting Europe and Asia, with Central Asia playing a key role. The BRI also includes investments in infrastructure in Africa and Asia.

---

[2]Bogetic, Željko, et al., 'Navigating troubled waters: The Red Sea shipping crisis and its global repercussions', *World Bank Blogs*, 16 May 2024. https://tinyurl.com/3c3v56s2. Accessed on 25 September 2024.

[3]Ibid.

According to some reports, investments to the tune of $1 trillion were made or planned.[4]

However, despite being more than a decade into its functioning, the BRI has not entirely been a success. Some projects have succeeded, but at the same time there has been criticism. The first strain of arguments centres around the fact that developing economies are saddled with debt far more than their capacity. Higher interest rates, shorter tenures, and collateralization significantly raise the cost of debt. Sri Lanka's default on the Hambantota Port in 2017 and Zambia's default in 2020 are oft-cited examples. Some authors have termed this 'debt-trap diplomacy' and assert that debt is used as leverage for geopolitical gains.[5] However, others insist that the real failure of BRI lies in the poor effectiveness of spending. In Kenya, for example, railroads worth billions of dollars that lead nowhere were built. Construction flaws have been found in a large-scale hydroelectric dam in Ecuador. Countries including Malaysia, Kazakhstan, Costa Rica, Ethiopia and Zambia have come forward to cancel or suspend projects in recent years.[6]

It is in this context that the IMEC, announced on the sidelines of the G20 Leaders' Summit in New Delhi, gains prominence. In addition to India, the US, EU, France, Germany, Italy, the UAE and Saudi Arabia are signatories to this corridor.

This grand connectivity project has been envisioned in two sections. The Eastern Corridor, which is inspired by the ancient trading routes, will connect India to the Gulf region, while a

[4]Wang, Christoph Nedopil, 'China Belt and Road Initiative (BRI) Investment Report 2023 H1', Green Finance and Development Center, 1 August 2023, https://tinyurl.com/mvrer5wd. Accessed on 25 September 2024.

[5]Chellaney, Brahma, 'China's Debt-Trap Diplomacy', *Project Syndicate*, 23 January 2017, https://tinyurl.com/28kuk29x. Accessed on 13 September 2024.

[6]Loh, Matthew, 'China spent twice as much as the US on overseas development, but its Belt and Road Initiative is losing momentum: study', *Business Insider*, 30 September 2021, https://tinyurl.com/yt5sk6p3. Accessed on 13 September 2024.

Northern Corridor will link the Gulf region to Europe through a railway and ship-rail transit network and road transport routes. The Indian ports of Kandla, Mundra and Mumbai and existing sea links to Fujairah, Jebel Ali and Abu Dhabi in the UAE will be leveraged. Goods will then move from railway lines traversing UAE and Saudi Arabia until they are offloaded at Haifa Port in Israel. From here, the goods will be transported by ship to the ports in Europe, where existing rail links will be leveraged and upgraded to move goods to their final destinations. These existing and proposed rail links, connecting ports on the Red Sea to ports in the Mediterranean Sea, are crucial to the success of IMEC. It has been estimated that this route between Europe and India could be 40 per cent faster than the Suez Canal route, owing to the use of high-speed trains. Also proposed for the corridor are cables for digital connectivity, pipelines for green hydrogen, and electric grid connectivity, making it not just about trade in goods.

The impact of such a corridor will be manifold. On a global macroeconomic level, the IMEC has the potential to secure regional supply chains. Individual nations will benefit immensely from increased access to trade and trade facilitation. Reduced costs and efficiencies will further boost trade, which will create growth and jobs in signatory nations.

Designed in partnership with the Partnership for Global Infrastructure and Investment (PGII), the IMEC, along with PGII, has been touted as a competitor to the BRI. The key difference between IMEC and BRI lies in the design. While the BRI is primarily designed to serve China's interests, in the case of the IMEC, the gains are distributed among the signatory nations. Each nation stands to benefit through trade and infrastructure development. Secondly, by bringing together creditor nations, and multilateral organizations, leveraging private investment, and building domestic capacities, developing countries will not be saddled with debt through IMEC. The IMEC has the potential to change the face of regional and global trade.

Global Biofuels Alliance: A Roadmap for Alternative Fuel

Whether trade is being conducted over land, sea, or air, what is common to all is the requirement of fuel. Most estimates peg the contribution of the transport sector at around a quarter of global CO2 emissions. At the same time, trade and growth have gone hand in hand. Estimates by the International Energy Agency (IEA) show that emissions from the transport sector must fall by three per cent annually until 2030 to achieve a net-zero scenario for 2050. On the other hand, the data shows that emissions from the transport sector have been growing at 1.7 per cent annually over the past 30 years.[7]

For countries such as India, which still have a large part of their growth ahead of them, there must be adequate room for growth. Decarbonizing the transport sector requires a multiplicity of solutions. Electric vehicles (EVs) are something India is aggressively pushing for in cities. Green hydrogen is another potential avenue for long-haul transport decarbonization, such as shipping and aviation.

Biofuels—essentially fuels made from plant materials, or biomass—can also play an important role in reducing emissions, according to the IEA. Two types of biofuels are most popular in the world today: bioethanol and biodiesel. Both fuels are blended with traditional fossil fuels such as petrol or diesel, which leads to lower emissions from vehicles. The most common sources to produce biofuels today are sugar or corn. India has also recognized

[7]Transport, *IEA 50*, https://tinyurl.com/4rek3vt4. Accessed on 25 September 2024.

the importance of biofuels in reducing import dependence and emissions. Our target of 20 per cent ethanol blending by 2030 has been brought forward to 2025.

The establishment of the Global Biofuels Alliance (GBA) is yet another significant legacy of India's G20 presidency. The GBA will bring together the biggest consumers and producers of biofuels. Twenty-four countries and 12 IOs have signed the GBA. These include Brazil and the US, two of the biggest producers and consumers of biofuels, France, Singapore and Argentina, as well as South Africa, who will take over the G20 presidency in December 2024.

One of the GBA's key areas of intervention will be setting standards. Varying international standards of biofuel blending, for instance, can hamper the trade of biofuels amongst nations. One of the challenges to expanding biofuel production has been the concern about the impact on the production of food crops, and deforestation. These concerns are being addressed by the JCC through the introduction of strong certification standards and exploring alternative inputs.

Proactive Action on Climate and SDG Finance

India also played a leading role in defining the urgency of action on climate and SDG finance.

At a side event of the second Sherpa meeting in Kumarakom, Dr Jeffrey Sachs, a world-renowned economics professor and global leader in sustainable development, put forward an ambitious agenda for climate and SDG finance. In his talk, he covered reasons why the present international financial system 'fails badly' to finance SDGs and climate goals. He made it clear that the developing world needed more long-term loans, at concessional rates, backed by a strong debt management framework.

Avinash Persaud, Special Envoy to the Prime Minister of Barbados, made an interesting case for unlocking financing for development. Presenting the Bridgetown Initiative, Persaud called for a reshaping of the global financial order to unlock an additional $2 trillion credit by 2030 to bridge the SDG investment gap.[8] Both these distinguished scholars and policy professionals clarified that the persistent financing gap for SDGs and climate was a binding constraint towards achieving our collective goals.

While the negotiations in Kumarakom had not yet started in earnest, this side event made one thing amply clear to our team—the conversation had to shift from billions to trillions of dollars. The scale of finance needed meant that private capital had to be leveraged. And the key to this scale-up would be the MDBs. However, 2023 was the first time the scale of finance and the needs of developing countries being put forward forthrightly reflected the way the global multilateral order had been functioning.

India's leadership championed innovative approaches within the Finance Track. Strengthening MDBs, advancing financial inclusion through DPI and cryptocurrencies, financing cities of tomorrow, managing global debt vulnerabilities, enhancing tax transparency and capacity building, and mobilizing climate and SDG finance were some of the key achievements of India's leadership in the Finance Track. India took charge of the challenging sovereign debt burden of low-income countries within the Common Framework and created a new mechanism of discussion on global debt in the form of the Global Sovereign Debt Roundtable. Strong US backing propelled these efforts, building on the Capital Adequacy Framework to enhance MDB capital efficiency. India leveraged prior work on climate finance

---

[8]The Bridgetown Initiative is a proposal to reform the world of development finance, particularly how rich countries help poor countries cope with and adapt to climate change.

and engaged an Independent Expert Group (IEG) to review the future role of the MDBs. Credit goes to Finance Minister Nirmala Sitharaman for taking the lead in constituting this committee. Her leadership during the presidency was pragmatic and forward-looking, with the Global South at the centre. She brought attention to the challenges faced by developing nations while aligning with global priorities. The full impact of this work will only be felt in the years to come, and her vision has undoubtedly made this a reality.

N.K. Singh and Larry Summers chaired the IEG. Singh is one of India's most distinguished economists, while Larry Summers is a prominent economist recognized for his influential work in government, macroeconomic policy and global finance. In two volumes, the IEG called for a new 'triple mandate' for the MDBs. Along with ending poverty and fostering socio-economic development, the report calls for MDBs to adopt an additional mandate of contributing to global public goods (GPGs). The group took a broad view of GPGs, encompassing climate change, biodiversity and pandemic preparedness, amongst others.

The reports from the G20 Independent Expert Group underscore the urgent need for an additional $3 trillion in annual investment by 2030 to achieve the SGDs and address climate challenges. This figure comprises $1.8 trillion for climate action and $1.2 trillion for other SDGs like health and education; approximately $2 trillion should come from domestic sources, while $1 trillion will require external financing, with MDBs playing a central role in mobilizing both public and private capital. To facilitate this massive investment, the international development finance system is called upon to provide $500 billion in additional annual official external financing by 2030. Furthermore, the reports highlight the necessity of mobilizing and catalyzing an equivalent amount of private capital, adding another $500 billion annually, thereby creating a total external financing package of $1 trillion. MDBs are expected to play a pivotal role by providing an incremental $260 billion of additional annual official financing, with $200 billion in non-concessional lending.

The reports also stress that international financial institutions, including MDBs, must reform themselves to meet these unprecedented financing needs. To do so, they should optimize balance sheets, use innovative financing mechanisms like hybrid capital, and adopt bolder strategies for engaging with the private sector. They recommend restructuring MDB operations to focus on multi-year, country-led platforms that streamline processes, address local conditions, and maximize the impact of investments. Additionally, the reports emphasize the need for MDBs to collaborate more effectively as a system, pool risks, and share diagnostic tools. The World Bank and other institutions have been urged to expand concessional financing, particularly for low-income and middle-income countries, to help them deliver global public goods and respond to global challenges such as climate change, pandemic preparedness, and biodiversity preservation.

While the IEG focused specifically on MDBs, the next step of reforms, aimed at the broader international financial architecture, must be initiated at the earliest. The IMF in their July 2024 World Economic Outlook project emerging and developing economies to grow at twice the rate than advanced economies in 2024 and 2025. Looking ahead, in the next 20–30 years the bulk of growth will come from developing markets. Various international panels, including the G20 Eminent Persons Group on Global Financial Architecture and the UN Secretary General's High-Level Advisory Panel, have highlighted the inadequacies of the global financial system in providing timely and scalable financing to these nations. Countries like India and Indonesia, for instance, do not have access to US dollar swap lines, forcing them to self-insure by accumulating large reserves, funds that could otherwise be directed towards growth and development. A strengthened and reformed IMF is crucial in addressing these liquidity gaps. To provide substantial liquidity beyond its current capabilities, the IMF needs to rethink its role, particularly concerning systemic central bank swap lines.[9]

The Sustainable Finance Working Group, co-chaired by the US and China, emphasized mobilizing resources for climate finance. India's Finance Track initiatives highlighted the importance of multilateral cooperation to address both legacy and emerging challenges in an interconnected global economy.

Reimagining Engagement Groups

Another key contribution was the active involvement of EGs, which played a crucial role in creating a lasting impact. As one of G20's most prominent EGs, the B20 played a crucial role in the deliberations as the voice of the global business community. The veritable who's who of India's business world came forward to make B20 India the most ambitious event in recent history. They ensured that the success of the G20 was not driven by the government alone. N. Chandrasekaran, Chairman of the Board of Tata Sons, was nominated as B20 India's Chair. He did a phenomenal job of leading B20 India. I have always admired his drive and dynamism, which he brought to the table at B20 India. He was visionary and forward-looking. It was under his leadership, and that of the Steering Committee consisting of Sanjiv Bajaj, Sanjiv Goenka and Milind Kamble, that B20 India emerged with one of the most ambitious B20 communiques in recent history. The Confederation of Indian Industry (CII), led by Chandrajit Banerjee and assisted by Neerja Bhatia, came

[9]Kant, Amitabh, and Siddharth Tiwari, 'Developing countries can spur global growth but they need support', *The Indian Express*, 20 June 2024, https://tinyurl.com/4zk25b85. Accessed on 9 December 2024.

forward as the secretariat of the B20 and did an exemplary job.

B20 India worked through seven task forces:

- Inclusive GVCs for resilient trade and development, which was led by Mallika Srinivasan, Chairperson & MD, TAFE India
- The future of work, skilling and mobility, led by Shobana Kamineni, Executive Vice Chairperson, Apollo Hospitals
- Sajjan Jindal, Chairman, JSW Group, led the energy, climate change and resource efficiency task force
- N. Chandrasekaran himself chaired the task force on digital transformation, such was his dedication
- Uday Kotak led the deliberations on financing for global economic recovery
- Kris Gopalakrishnan led the tech, innovation and R&D task force
- The financial inclusion for economic empowerment taskforce was led by Dinesh Kumar Khara, then chairperson of SBI

In addition, B20 India set up two Action Councils (ACs) on Environment, Social and Governance (ESG) in Business and African Economic Integration.

These groundbreaking ideas, solutions and actionable recommendations of B20 India were consolidated in the 'B20 India Communique' with 54 recommendations and 172 policy enablers. Out of all these recommendations, we incorporated almost all in some form or the other in the NDLD. One of the key long-term recommendations to come out of B20 India is the establishment of a permanent B20 Institute, which has been taken forward, as well as a Global SDG Acceleration Fund.

The Think20 (T20) engagement group serves as the G20's 'ideas bank'. With 131 members, across 7 task forces, from

88 international and 37 Indian institutions, India had one of the largest think tank exercises since the T20 first began. Credit goes to Sujan R. Chinoy, Director General of Manohar Parrikar Institute for Defence Studies and Analyses (MP-IDSA), who chaired T20 India, and Samir Saran, President, Observer Research Foundation (ORF), who drove such an ambitious agenda.

The T20, unlike Business20 or Women20 and other targeted engagement groups, has plural perspectives. This was crucial as the final leaders' statement would have to reflect a plurality of views. Moreover, the T20 had to present solutions that accommodated all the diverse viewpoints keeping in mind the full spectrum of stakeholders, not just business or civil society.

T20 India was able to create coherence out of this plurality. Over 300 policy briefs and other research products were produced by 1,000 authors from over 700 institutions. The authors were from 75 countries, with 42 per cent of them being women, ensuring both gender and geographical diversity.

As part of the outreach and stakeholder engagement, 64 convenings were held across 16 Indian cities and six abroad. T20 India linked the G20 process with existing multilateral frameworks like the United Nations General Assembly (UNGA), the spring meetings of the World Bank, and COP28. Through meetings on the sidelines of these events, T20 drew attention to specific recommendations on climate finance, extending G20 membership to the AU, and creating a better understanding of DPI, and Lifestyles for Sustainable Development. To ensure continuity in the development conversation, India and Brazil conducted the T20 handover in South Africa at a flagship event of the Global South, the Cape Town Conversation.

Civil20 was another crucial engagement group that resonated with our attempts to make our G20 presidency a 'people's presidency'. It was led by Sri Mata Amritanandamayi Devi, known as Amma—the first spiritual leader to be nominated to chair a G20 engagement group, another unique facet of India's presidency. The goal of C20 was to ensure that the voices from all strata of society are reflected in the G20. The Civil 20 policy pack is the result of a staggering 1,300 in-person or online meetings with 6,000 delegates from 154 countries. Under Amma's leadership, C20 India's outreach touched 4.5 million people, the highest ever in the history of C20.

Parliament20 is another unique aspect of the G20 process, providing a different dimension to G20 discussions. Led by Speaker of the Lok Sabha, Om Birla, it brought together the leaders of the parliaments of G20 nations, where a joint statement recognized India's ancient tradition of people's participation in decision-making and governance.

Celebrating our Agricultural Heritage

India's G20 presidency marked a significant shift in global culinary and agricultural focus, with millets—traditional nutritious grains—taking centre stage. The International Year of Millets (IYM) 2023, recognized by the UNGA, gave India a platform to globalize this superfood's advantages, reflecting a commitment to sustainable agriculture and nutrition. Under PM Modi's initiative to rebrand millets as 'Shree Anna', their promotion was a prominent theme throughout G20-related events. As a leader in millet production and export, we wanted to use our presidency as a platform to share India's traditional wisdom on millets with the world. Apart from showcasing our rich culinary heritage, this move was part of a longer-term strategy to integrate these climate-smart, ancient grains into healthier and more sustainable global food practices.

We wanted to add a visceral vitality to the discussions, to remind leaders what was at stake was real lives and livelihoods, and that our championship of millets was based on sound science—the fact that millets are versatile and taste delicious was the icing on the cake. Top chefs from leading hotels crafted innovative millet dishes, introducing delegates to the grain's versatility and nutritional value. Throughout the year, delegates had the opportunity to try various millet-based dishes—from savoury biryanis to sweet puddings—each unique to the regional cuisine of the state they were visiting. Specialties like ragi and *litti chokha* not only tantalized the taste buds but also sparked conversations about the revival of a crop that had been cultivated for millennia yet overshadowed by other grains since the colonial era. Dishes like bajra and ragi malt and *gajar halwa* cake with saffron mascarpone showcased the grain's culinary versatility while highlighting India's commitment to climate-resilient agriculture. These efforts eventually led to several cookbooks that further popularized millets.

Parallel to the culinary celebrations, our presidency launched the MAHARISHI initiative, a Sanskrit acronym for 'Millets and Other Ancient Grains International Research Initiative'. This ambitious project aimed to bolster research and awareness surrounding agro-biodiversity, food security and nutrition, aligning perfectly with IYM 2023. MAHARISHI's goals included enhancing food security and nutrition while strengthening agricultural resilience, promoting digital transformation in agriculture, and fostering public-private partnerships.

Despite the linguistic challenges and pushback from some G20 members to the use of the Sanskrit acronym in international documents, India's commitment to this initiative remained steadfast. The focus was on collaborative research and knowledge sharing on millets and other underutilized grains, and identifying information gaps and needs.

As world leaders converged in New Delhi for the G20 Summit, we arranged a special visit to the Indian Agricultural Research

Institute (IARI) campus in New Delhi on 9 September for the spouses of the G20 leaders. The focus was on highlighting India's strides in agriculture, particularly the significance of millets. The visit included a tour of millet fields where rows and rows of slender, sturdy stalks, about the thickness of a pencil, stretched their fingers skywards.

The field visit also included an exhibition featuring 'Agriculture Street', an immersive journey through India's agricultural heritage, blending ancient practices with modern advancements. Interactive stalls guided the visitors through the various stages of cultivation, focusing on millets and the rich genetic diversity of India's crops. Guests marvelled at the innovative agri-startups on display, each showcasing unique, tech-based solutions to combat modern-day agricultural challenges. The exhibition also emphasized the role of women in agriculture with women farmers from 11 millet-producing states sharing their experiences. These states have been at the forefront of revolutionizing millet production, showcasing India's efforts in boosting the cultivation, processing, marketing and consumption of millets.

An unforgettable moment was the live cooking demonstration, where renowned chefs highlighted the versatility of millets in various cuisines. Dishes from all G20 member countries were served. Artistic creations like millet-based *rangoli*s adorned the venue. The rangolis, themed 'Harmony of Harvest' and 'The World Is One Family', embodied the spirit of shared global responsibility.

The leaders of G20 nations were treated to a special menu featuring diverse flavours of India, with millets as the hero ingredient. The highlight of this culinary extravaganza was the gala dinner hosted by President Droupadi Murmu. A stunning three-course vegetarian feast was served that evening, celebrating the 'autumn season of abundance'. Each millet dish, specific in its size, taste and coarseness, spoke of the soil on which it was grown, showing, rather than telling, leaders of the unbreakable links between agricultural practices, local ecosystems and cultural identities.

Cultural Cauldron

India's G20 presidency was perhaps the only one where the cultural and creative industries were recognized as drivers of inclusive growth in the Leaders' Declaration. The G20 Culture Ministers adopted the Kashi Culture Pathway ahead of the Leaders' Summit. Former Culture Secretary Govind Mohan and his team worked tirelessly, driving consensus on this pathway. They also played a pivotal role throughout the year to ensure all G20 delegates experienced India's rich, vibrant and diverse culture.

The closing ceremony for the Bharat Mandapam had originally been proposed for open-air venues like Kartavya Path and the Red Fort, but due to weather concerns and the threat of rain, PM Modi made the decisive choice to hold it at Bharat Mandapam, transforming it into a venue that will hold historical significance forever.

We reimagined the traditional gala dinner as *Ratribhoj Par Samvaad* (Conversation over Dinner), allowing for a relaxed interaction that worked beautifully for all leaders. This new format created an environment of fellowship, breaking down barriers while encouraging genuine connection.

To create a truly immersive experience for guests, a series of exhibitions were organized to showcase India's technological advancements and cultural richness.

One of the most exciting elements was the 'Culture Corridor: G20 Digital Museum'. This initiative celebrated the shared heritage of the G20 nations, featuring iconic cultural artefacts that told stories of diverse identities and traditions. Thanks to the sterling work done by Lily Pandeya, the exhibition became a vibrant platform that fostered understanding and unity among participants.

India integrated a cultural undercurrent into the global conversation by introducing a 'Crafts Bazaar' at the Bharat Mandapam. This unique event, featuring the craftsmanship of items like *Kolhapuri* chappals and *Paithani* saris from Maharashtra, reflected India's commitment to offering a global stage to local artisans while celebrating India's rich heritage, particularly through the lens of the One District One Product (ODOP) initiative.

By focusing on ODOP, the initiative also fostered economic opportunities, opening new markets for artisans by offering international delegates a firsthand experience of India's rich cultural and craft traditions. The Crafts Bazaar, a collaborative effort between the G20 Secretariat and the Ministry of Textiles, exemplified how the G20 Summit transformed host cities into vibrant cultural hubs. To add a personal touch to the G20 experience, each host city included an ODOP item in delegate gift bags. These thoughtfully curated bags offered delegates a tangible connection to India's diverse local craftsmanship, and by featuring ODOP items, the host cities became ambassadors of the economic potential of local artisans.

Beyond its role in bringing local cultural traditions and handicraft practices to the global forefront, reinforcing a regional focus for the G20, India generated meaningful employment opportunities for artisans across diverse communities.

The Digital India Experience Zone presented key initiatives like Aadhaar and UPI, which illustrated India's strides in modern technology. At the RBI's Innovation Pavilion, leaders explored cutting-edge financial technologies that showcased how India was reshaping its financial landscape.

Each of these aspects was a representation of India's diverse culture and commitment to creating global relationships that were more than transactional. By sharing bits and pieces of Indian culture, PM Modi invited world leaders into a deeper understanding of India's heritage, values and traditions—the pillars that guide our outlook on the past as well as the future.

EIGHT

LEADERSHIP IN ACTION: WHAT I LEARNT FROM PM MODI

On 1 December 2022, the day India took over the G20 presidency, the energy within Sushma Swaraj Bhawan was electric, marked by excitement and a shared sense of purpose. However, the groundwork for the G20 Summit had already been laid much earlier, driven by PM Modi's vision for India's leadership.

The prime minister's vision for a human-centric and interconnected world formed the backbone of India's G20 agenda. In his influential speech in Bali, PM Modi called for a departure from zero-sum international relations. Drawing on India's spiritual heritage, he proposed the theme Vasudhaiva Kutumbakam, 'One Earth, One Family, One Future,' emphasizing global unity and shared destiny.

This concept drove a significant change in mindset within the G20 Secretariat, influencing daily operations and strategy. PM Modi envisioned moving past historical conflicts and encouraged a united effort to tackle challenges like climate change, terrorism and pandemics. He believed in humanity's ability to use modern technology for global problem-solving, marking it as the cornerstone of India's presidency.

The global pandemic solidified his belief that a drastic change in the world's civilizational value system was long overdue. It was time to stop viewing opportunities solely in terms of economic value, and to shift from a GDP-centric approach to a human-centric perspective—one that places people over profit and brings prosperity and well-being to all of humanity.

This philosophy has been a cornerstone of India's diplomatic worldview since 2014 when PM Modi introduced the concept of a 'world as one family' during his historic address at the UN General Assembly. In his speech, he emphasized the need to increase the influence of the G4 coalition and urged the international community to move away from the perception of policy as a 'zero-sum game.'[1]

Reforming the UN is central to realizing this vision, enabling a more inclusive global governance structure that reflects the diverse needs and aspirations of all nations. In his address on the commemoration of the 75th anniversary of the UN in 2020, PM Modi asserted that 'only reformed multilateralism with a reformed United Nations at its centre can meet the aspirations of humanity.'[2]

This framework raises the question: if humanity's problems are interconnected, how can international bodies solve them with 1.4 billion people missing from critical conversations? India is among many countries advocating for its rightful place in the global dialogue. Excluding significant populations from the discussion undermines the legitimacy of these conversations and perpetuates a narrow worldview that cannot address global challenges. To effectively tackle issues like climate change, poverty and health crises, international organizations need to ensure that all voices are heard, particularly those from rapidly developing nations. In the realm of climate change, this is poignant—oceans and winds don't recognize man-made borders. PM Modi's vision of human-centric globalization reminds us we share the same planet, and its destruction is our destruction.

'We are committed to a sustainable path to prosperity,' the PM stated at the Sustainable Development Summit in New York on 25 September 2015. 'It comes from the instinct of our tradition and culture. But it is also rooted firmly in our commitment to

---

[1]Full text of PM Modi's speech at UNGA, *Business Standard*, https://tinyurl.com/34cvcukd. Accessed on 14 September 2024.

[2]'At UN meet, PM Modi calls for "reformed multilateralism"', *The Hindu*, 17 July 2020, https://tinyurl.com/yze5dvpj. Accessed on 14 September 2024.

the future. We represent a culture that calls our planet Mother Earth,' he added.[3]

A just and sustainable transition is essential to ensure that all nations—especially those most vulnerable to environmental degradation—are equipped to adapt and thrive. This requires equitable access to technology transfers that enable developing nations to embrace renewable energy and sustainable practices, along with robust financial support to enhance resilience to climate impacts.

In this complex world of global diplomacy, where uncertainty often overshadows optimism, India's G20 presidency unfolded as a remarkable chapter. Under PM Modi, a sense of hope resonated through the G20 India team. The task was enormous—steering through conflicts like Russia-Ukraine and tackling climate and energy transitions all rested on India's shoulders.

Despite these obstacles, an indomitable purpose propelled us forward. Prime Minister Modi believed in the impossible, trusting his team to prioritize the development of India and the Global South, and fight for our planet's longevity.

The Prime Minister's leadership style laid the foundation of optimism, trust in our creative solutions, and stoic resilience. His unshakeable faith in our team kept us determined. He had delegated a lot and had faith in me, and therefore, it was incumbent upon me to deliver. His presidency showed that with hope and a clear vision, obstacles become opportunities to bring about lasting change and rewrite the narrative of global diplomacy.

---

[3]Statement by Prime Minister Shri Narendra Modi at the Sustainable Development Summit New York, on 25 September 2015, https://tinyurl.com/5d2abpp5. Accessed on 14 September 2024.

Sabka Saath: Towards an Inclusive Global Order

Of all the key factors that made the eventual success of the NDLD possible, solidarity from the Global South was a central factor. PM Modi recognized the pronounced imbalance in multilateral representation between the Global North and South early on and saw the G20 presidency as an opportunity to correct this historical bias. The Global South—a vulnerable majority without a voice—had been overlooked for too long, and the PM was certain that 'we should also have an equivalent voice.'[4]

India's role in various international groupings has been integral to this diplomatic strategy. As a founding member of BRICS, India reaffirmed its commitment to emerging markets, while its active participation in QUAD with the US, Japan and Australia showcased its dedication to regional security and economic cooperation. Notably, India resisted China's repeated overtures to join the BRI in 2017, a decision that shows its desire for strategic autonomy and its focus on sustainable partnerships.

Throughout these diplomatic initiatives, PM Modi's leadership style focused on creating space for emerging economies within the existing frameworks, as well as advocating reforms that would grant developing nations a greater role in shaping the global agenda.

Just before the G20 Summit in India, PM Modi also attended the ASEAN-India and East Asia summits in Jakarta. There, he emphasized the importance of creating a rules-based order in the post-COVID-19 landscape, particularly considering China's increasing claims of territorial disputes. He expressed a commitment to strengthening the sovereignty and territorial integrity of all nations. During the ASEAN-India Summit, he proposed a 12-point

---

[4]Haidar, Suhasini, 'Winds of change in global governance | Global South', *The Hindu,* 17 September 2023, https://tinyurl.com/dvf9rvj9. Accessed on 14 September 2024.

plan to enhance cooperation, reinforcing the idea that India would work alongside ASEAN members to amplify the voices of the Global South and secure a free and open Indo-Pacific.

By building lasting connections with the global community, and instilling trust in India's vision, the PM made my job as Sherpa and our ability to arrive at consensus simpler and easier. In the end, the Global South stood firmly together. As a collective, this tetrad of developing countries—India, Brazil, South Africa and Indonesia—presented the final draft of the Leaders' Declaration as a common document, leveraging the weight of a united front with a common voice and shared interests. Backed by Saudi Arabia, Mexico, Argentina and Türkiye, the message was unambiguous: it was time for the developed world to be in a responding position; the agenda had been set for and by the emerging markets.

Great Leaders Take Great Risks

Leadership requires courage and a selfless commitment to service.[5] Great leaders are distinguished in part by their vision and decisiveness, but also by their willingness to take significant risks in pursuit of monumental goals. Such audacity is often the hallmark of transformative leadership.

The success of India's G20 presidency hinged on a leader unafraid to make history through calculated risks. Taking risks in leadership is not merely about navigating the known, but also about confronting the unknown. We faced numerous complexities as we navigated negotiations with influential players like the G7, Russia and China. The threat of isolation, conflicting interests, and the challenge of finding consensus increased the stakes, as fragile bilateral relationships hung in the balance.

---

[5]Balasubramaniam, R., *Power Within: The Leadership Legacy of Narendra Modi*, Penguin Random House India (2024).

Our boldness wasn't confined to the negotiation table. The willingness to explore alternative avenues, including potential collaboration with other global groupings such as IBSA and BRICS, showed a leader ready to pivot if the situation demanded. The risks were not taken lightly, but were embraced with the understanding that transformative change often required stepping into uncharted territory. And this territory included playing hardball with different countries during negotiations.

Faced with Russia's objections to certain terminology, we got all the emerging markets together, including building a personal relationship with China, leaving Russia with no choice. Our assertive tactics played a vital role in securing Russia's consent and averting their potential diplomatic isolation. We also proactively addressed China's visa-related concerns, demonstrating a readiness to confront challenges head-on, even when it was technically outside India's G20 mandate. This added complexity required deft navigation between China's requirements and maintaining a balanced rapport with the US. In the end, with all stakeholders finally aligned, India's big bets finally paid off.

History teaches us that transformative change often springs from bold choices. From President John F. Kennedy's firm stance during the Cuban Missile Crisis to Deng Xiaoping's sweeping economic reforms in China, decisive actions have left a lasting impact on the global landscape. India's G20 presidency adds to this legacy, highlighting how risk-taking can catalyze positive change. Prime Minister Modi's leadership exemplifies the enduring power of bold decisions in shaping a brighter and more inclusive future for all.

Effective and Dynamic Communication

The success of India's G20 presidency demonstrated the power of effective communication in its many forms. At its core, this strategy was not just about disseminating information but also about fostering a spirit of collective participation that resonated from grassroots levels all the way to the global stage.

The finest example of this is PM Modi himself, who has set the precedent for a regular, effective and dynamic communication style with the people of India. Whether through his radio programme *Mann Ki Baat*, his X engagement, where he hit 100 million followers in July 2024, or his personal interactions like *Pariksha Pe Charcha*, where he interacts with students and parents about exam stress and education, PM Modi's communication approach has transformed the dynamics of public discourse. His ability to connect with citizens on various platforms demonstrates a keen understanding of the diverse ways people consume information, ensuring that his messages resonate widely. By embracing multimedia, engaging directly with youth, and addressing pressing societal issues, he has built a culture of openness and accessibility, making governance feel more connected and relevant to people.

At the G20 Summit, a dedicated website and active social media channels provided real-time updates, resources, and a platform for interactive discussions with the general public. The virtual meetings, data and resources, expertly curated for the first time during India's tenure, left a solid foundation for Brazil, allowing for the seamless transition of working material, and ensuring continuity and sustained global dialogue beyond geographical constraints. This technological integration reflects G20 India's commitment to transparency, accessibility, innovation, and continuing collaboration in the digital age.

Internal communication played a crucial role in ensuring effective coordination between central and state authorities, exemplifying cooperative federalism. Logistical synchronization, which is crucial for seamless execution, demands efficient communication channels. Negotiating with diverse stakeholders, both domestically and internationally, required a nuanced grasp of various cultures and languages. Our team constantly adapted to local laws while pivoting to engage on the international stage, navigating multiple time zones and shifting the focus from minutiae—like names on placards and the preparation of regional cuisines—to macro concerns such as climate-smart agriculture, health technology, and global energy transition.

That Personal Touch

Maya Angelou once wisely said, 'People will forget what you said, people will forget what you did, but people will never forget how you made them feel.'

I have always understood the importance of branding. Perceptions create realities, and these realities form the bedrock of almost every action known to humankind. It's the story we remember. The emotion it evokes stays with us long after the facts have faded.

One of my transformative experiences came during my tenure as the Tourism Secretary of Kerala from 1997 to 2001. This period was a blessing in many ways. I partnered in Kerala's incredible journey from an unknown destination to India's No. 1 tourism hotspot. When I moved to the Ministry of Tourism in Delhi in late 2001, I faced an immense challenge—holding the vast canvas of India together with one powerful idea that could unify the nation as an aspirational destination. After nearly a year of research, debates and public consultations, that idea took shape as Incredible India! Over six years, this campaign transformed India into one of the world's top destinations, recognized by the *Condé Nast Traveler* Readers' Choice Award in 2007.

An idea is an incredibly powerful thing. In the mid-2000s, even climate change needed a publicist. Despite the undeniable evidence and the significant implications for the future of the planet, the scientific community's warnings were initially met with widespread scepticism and apathy. The message was mired in complex jargon and lacked the compelling narrative needed to resonate with the public. It wasn't until communicators like Al Gore used gripping visuals and relatable stories in his documentary *An Inconvenient Truth* that the message penetrated the public consciousness more effectively. His approach transformed the perception of climate change from a distant, abstract concept to an urgent, personal call to action.

PM Modi understood this better than anyone else. As the spokesperson of the Global South, India's G20 campaign had to be memorable in more ways than one. This was an opportunity to showcase the cultural and societal diversity that informed our policy strengths. With this vision, the G20 presidency highlighted the invaluable contributions of local artisans, craftspeople and women entrepreneurs. Their involvement in the international conference was vital, bringing a slice of India's rich heritage directly to the global stage.

Staying true to the spirit of *Atithi Devo Bhava*, all delegates and guests were warmly welcomed at the airport with traditional greetings and presented with local handmade sweets at their hotels—a personal touch that made for some truly Insta-worthy moments! They experienced the heart of India, a refreshing contrast to the narratives often portrayed by foreign media outlets, showcasing the warmth and richness of our culture. This hospitality left a lasting impression, reinforcing India's commitment to friendship and collaboration.

In the same spirit, we had planned an elaborate menu with multi-course meals and multiple cultural programmes for the banquet PM Modi would host for the G20 leaders. When we presented our ideas to him, he was of a different view. He mentioned that he had attended several G20 events, multilateral gatherings and banquets. At the end of the day, the attendees are tired and eager to network with others. Often, leaders only stay for a short time before leaving, which means they miss out on the chance for meaningful interactions. He asked us not to organize anything elaborate or extravagant. The meals were simple, with soft music playing in the background. The difference was evident: during our dinner, most leaders stayed until the end, taking the time to socialize and spend time with each other. Many ambassadors appreciated the break from tradition. This again reflected PM Modi's personal touch to the event. As a gesture of goodwill and cultural exchange, PM Modi presented to the dignitaries attending the G20 Summit carefully selected gifts reflecting India's rich heritage. Among the gifts was a stunning Banarasi stole made of silk threads and intricately woven, which embodied the cultural richness of Varanasi; Sundarbans multiflora mangrove honey, sourced from the world's largest mangrove forest and known for its rich flavour and health benefits; Araku coffee, a distinctive product hailed as the world's first terroir-mapped coffee, grown in the organic plantations of the Araku Valley in Andhra Pradesh; Pekoe-Darjeeling and Nilgiri Tea, celebrated for its exquisite taste and aroma and often referred to as the 'Champagne of Teas'; and Zighrana attar, an ancient perfume from Kannauj that evokes memories of royal courts and traditional bazaars, adding a sensory delight to the gift collection.

The PM presented the Banarasi stole to the wife of Spanish Prime Minister Pedro Sánchez, María Begoña Gómez Fernández, in a beautifully crafted ebony wood *jali* box, showcasing the exquisite craftsmanship of artisans of Kerala. For the wife of Brazilian President Luiz Inácio Lula da Silva, Rosangela da Silva, PM Modi presented a luxurious pashmina stole. To Mauritius PM Pravind Jugnauth's wife, Kobita Ramdanee, the PM presented an Ikat stole, a traditional mulberry silk stole from Odisha, crafted using the unique Ikat technique. It was complemented by a handcrafted teakwood box from Gujarat.

Honouring Every Contribution

For PM Modi, the success of India's G20 presidency wasn't just about successfully hosting an event, but also in creating a lasting real-world impact. As soon as we achieved success, he visited Sushma Swaraj Bhawan, engaging directly with young officers to gather their valuable input. Attributing the success of the G20 to the entire country, he exemplified a leadership style that values collaboration and recognizes the collective efforts of the nation. This direct and inclusive approach reflects the PM's commitment to involving all stakeholders and fostering a sense of shared achievement.

Soon after, PM Modi interacted with over 3,000 ground-level G20 functionaries at the Bharat Mandapam. During this engagement, he uncovered a trove of stories that displayed the dedication, innovation and sacrifice of G20 workers that transcended mere duty. From sub-inspector Pinky Rani's ingenious use of the G20 App to overcome a language barrier to inspector Suresh Kumar's decision to uphold national duty amid personal adversity, these narratives epitomized the meticulous planning and collective commitment that made the summit a success. Pravin Kumar's midnight efforts to repair damaged flowerpots and Ravinder Tyagi's wife expressing pride in his G20 participation added depth to the narrative, underscoring the pivotal role that these unsung heroes played in the historic event. The PM's interactions illuminated the human side of the Summit's triumph, portraying individuals who went the extra mile to contribute to the nation's pride. Recognizing the long-term value of collective memory, the PM emphasized the need to document experiences, turning them into invaluable guidelines for future events.

Upon closely listening to PM Modi's address to the G20 team, five distinct leadership qualities emerged, shedding light on his unique approach to governance.

First and foremost was the consistent emphasis on collective effort, portraying a leader who attributed success to the combined contributions of the entire team rather than individual achievements.

Secondly, recognizing the relentless hard work of the diverse G20 team underscored a leadership style that valued dedication and persistent effort.

Thirdly, PM Modi's call for a more relaxed and inclusive environment suggested a departure from traditional bureaucratic norms, showcasing a leader who sought the contribution of all lower ranks, particularly grassroots functionaries.

Fourthly, the encouragement to share experiences informally highlighted a leader who fostered open communication and valued the insights of each team member. Furthermore, his insistence on documenting experiences for future reference indicated a commitment to continuous improvement and a leader who learnt from past endeavours.

Lastly, a focus on the cumulative impact of collective efforts indicated a leader who was more interested in lasting results than momentary acclaim.

Beyond the praise, his true joy lay in the nation's growing confidence, exemplified by India's contributions to the global rescue. In his interaction with the ground-level functionaries, the PM's focus was not on accolades but on instilling the belief that the country could confidently host any such event. This acknowledgement of collective effort and genuine appreciation of hard work underscored the PM's leadership style—blending vision with authentic recognition of dedication.

In the face of global challenges, PM Modi's can-do approach

became a guiding force, instilling confidence in India's capabilities. Confronting obstacles head-on, the nation exhibited resilience and creativity, reflecting the qualities essential for effective leadership. The Prime Minister's hands-on approach and emphasis on hard work underscored the indispensable role of diligence in achieving success. Taking diplomatic risks showcased a leader unafraid of challenges and willing to make bold moves for the greater good. Focusing on building a competent team, particularly by harnessing the energy of young minds, exemplified the power of collective leadership. Ultimately, the strategic use of communication—both digital and physical—proved to be the backbone of India's successful global engagement.

India's G20 presidency stands as a rich source of lessons in visionary leadership, resilience, and the art of effective communication, inspiring our G20 team and promising to guide the next generation of leaders.

Lessons of a Lifetime

Few leaders in the world can change the air of the room when they walk into it. It is undeniable that PM Modi is one such person. In the years I have worked with him, I have seen him display equal levels of strategic acumen and empathetic leadership, effortlessly balancing the two in ways that encourage people to think, feel and, most importantly, act.

Firstly, he always approaches challenges with a long-term perspective, considering the broader implications of each decision amongst a host of possible realities. Whether in ministerial presentations or official meetings, I have watched him dissect complex issues with a clarity that allows for innovative solutions. At the same time, his profound empathy shapes the way he engages with people from all walks of life. He listens intently, making everyone feel valued and understood—a quality that builds bridges across turbulent waters.

This duality of intellect and heart inspired me to cultivate a similar balance in my approach to leadership. I have learnt that effective leadership is not just about making decisions, but also about nurturing relationships and creating spaces where others feel empowered to share their thoughts and ideas. PM Modi's ability to command a room while ensuring every voice is heard is a lesson I carry with me, influencing the way I engage with peers and collaborators alike.

Secondly, the most striking aspect of PM Modi's leadership is his discipline in listening. He spends an astonishing 95 per cent of his time listening, dedicating nearly the entire hour of meetings to absorbing perspectives before contributing his own thoughts. During my time as his Sherpa, I emulated this firsthand as I spent 55 minutes of the hour-long conference listening to leaders from over twenty nations, international organizations, and guests. This practice goes beyond mere patience; it cultivates a deep understanding of what truly matters to people—their priorities, the sacrifices they are willing to make, and the issues they choose to emphasize or overlook. Only such understanding begets influence. When you genuinely listen, you begin to grasp the nuances of their positions, allowing you to connect on a deeper level and engage more meaningfully. This ability to discern not only enhanced collaboration but also empowered me to inspire actions aligned with shared goals and values. Listening transformed dialogue into a powerful tool for driving change.

Thirdly, PM Modi's remarkable calmness under pressure stands out. Throughout our numerous interactions, I never once saw him raise his voice or react angrily, regardless of the provocations he faced. This composure has taught me that strength is often found in restraint. He embodies resilience, demonstrating that true leadership involves holding firm in the face of external pressures and adversities without wavering.

As the G20 presidency progressed and the pressure mounted, especially in the final stages, it was crucial for us to believe in our vision for India. He showed me the importance of standing resilient against external pressures, encouraging a culture of perseverance within our team. His steadfastness encouraged me to remain resolute in my convictions, reinforcing that true leadership often involves weathering the storm without capitulating to the demands around you.

Fourthly, PM Modi's optimistic outlook encouraged a forward-thinking approach, reminding me that maintaining hope was essential to our pursuit of meaningful change. His faith in possibilities encouraged me to adopt a mindset where curiosity and resilience coexisted. Instead of viewing problems as definitive endpoints, I now see them as invitations to reevaluate our strategies and approaches.

Finally, his commitment to physical and mental well-being is evident in his practices of yoga and meditation. These disciplines helped me manage stress during periods of high-stakes policy work, allowing me to stay alert and present throughout the day. During intense geopolitical negotiations, where we often found ourselves burning the midnight oil, the strong foundation of health I cultivated through mindfulness practices proved invaluable. These habits of awareness and focus allowed me to remain fully engaged and attentive to the details of each country's edits and contributions. For the mind and body to absorb and impart new information, they must remain sponge-like: flexible, open, and able to both embrace and let go.

Working alongside PM Modi has been a transformative experience, one that continues to shape my professional outlook and personal growth. As I continue my journey, I strive to embody these invaluable lessons—listening deeply, maintaining composure, embodying resilience, nurturing optimism, and prioritizing well-being—allowing them to guide my engagements and contributions in a complex world.

EPILOGUE

SHARED GOALS, SHARED SUCCESSES

As India's G20 presidency drew to a successful close, I wrote a heartfelt letter to all Sherpas, expressing my deeply felt gratitude and appreciation for their constant support and collaboration since the presidency began on 1 December 2022. In this letter, I acknowledged their invaluable contributions, stating, 'Your thoughts, your suggestions, your flexibility, your friendship and your readiness to walk that extra mile, hand-in-hand and together with me, through thick and thin, is what made it possible for all of us to successfully adopt the G20 New Delhi Leaders' Declaration (NDLD) on 9 September 2023.'

I emphasized the collective effort and authorship behind the NDLD, recognizing the essential role each Sherpa and their team members played in its successful finalization. The success of the New Delhi G20 Summit, held at the grand Bharat Mandapam on 9–10 September 2023, was a testament to the strong leadership of both their leaders and our Prime Minister, Narendra Modi.

Reflecting on the achievements of the NDLD, I noted, 'By ensuring that the entire G20 spoke in one unified voice, on a wide range of global challenges, from geopolitical tensions to climate change to inclusive growth, the NDLD has not only helped keep G20 intact but has also made it stronger.' I also acknowledged the many concessions and exceptional flexibility shown by all the Sherpas, who were crucial in achieving the substantive outcomes of the NDLD while maintaining their respective national positions.

Toward the end, I expressed my appreciation for the friendships and bonds we developed during this journey. 'I will continue to cherish the long hours that we spent together debating, discussing, and occasionally sharing a much-required joke to lighten the intensity of our deliberations,' I wrote. I wished them and their families the best of health, success, prosperity and happiness, and looked forward to continuing our friendship and keeping in touch in the years to come.

The letter was a tribute to the spirit of collaboration and unity that defined our G20 presidency and to the shared commitment to address global challenges through multilateralism. Reflecting on the intense year we all underwent together, I cherished the realization that these were my peers, each dedicated to making the world a better place, even when we disagreed. As many of us will continue this journey in the coming year, I remain grateful for the friendships forged and the collective resolve to create positive change.

I would also like to extend my heartfelt thanks to my brilliant young colleagues, Rajeshwari Sahay, Nandita Singh, Soham Kshirsagar, and Abhishek Sudke, whose dedication and tireless efforts were instrumental in shaping India's G20 presidency. Ranveer Nagaich played a crucial role throughout the year, supporting me in shaping and drafting the NDLD. Their fresh perspectives, innovative ideas, and unwavering commitment played a vital role not only in the success of the presidency but also in bringing this book to life.

POSTSCRIPT

THE FUTURE OF MULTILATERALISM

The future of multilateralism is under threat. In the aftermath of World War II, the present form of multilateralism was designed to foster collective responses to global challenges. However, recent conflicts, climate crises, failure to achieve SDGs and growing nationalist tendencies threaten its relevance and effectiveness.

The resurgence of geopolitical conflicts, such as the war in Ukraine in February 2022, ongoing conflict in West Asia, including Israel's military actions in Gaza and Lebanon, and the Syrian civil war, have exposed the limits of multilateral institutions. The UNSC, historically tasked with maintaining global peace, has been paralyzed due to the veto power wielded by its permanent members. Competing geopolitical interests have turned multilateral platforms into arenas for blame-shifting rather than problem-solving. The result is a growing perception that multilateralism serves as a venue for political theatre rather than meaningful action. Rising nationalism and protectionism are further eroding multilateralism. The US-China economic rivalry has also spilled over into multilateral institutions, with both powers seeking to assert their dominance rather than pursue collective global solutions. Within the G20, we have seen bilateral issues spill over into multilateral negotiations, leading to gridlocks.

In the face of failing multilateralism, growing regionalism or smaller-scale arrangements and agreements are being turned to for addressing shared concerns. While regionalism has had positive effects—the EU and the AU, for instance—the effectiveness of multilateral institutions continues to be eroded. This is perhaps best exemplified by the erosion of the multilateral trading system as envisioned by the WTO. The WTO's dispute settlement mechanism remains paralyzed. Without a strong dispute resolution mechanism, protectionism and unilateral trade measures are increasingly on the rise. Before that, the failure of the Doha Development Round of negotiations left many developing countries disillusioned with the WTO. Countries are increasingly turning to regional and smaller trade agreements, bypassing the WTO system. Examples include the Comprehensive and Progressive Agreement for Trans-Pacific Partnership (CPTPP) and the Regional Comprehensive Economic Partnership (RCEP).

Multilateralism relies on political will and shared commitment, both of which are increasingly in short supply. The interconnected and transnational nature of today's challenges magnifies the inadequacies of traditional multilateralism. Take the issue of climate change, for instance. Recent events at the Conference of the Parties (COP) 29 in Baku, Azerbaijan, highlight perfectly the inadequacies and inequalities inherent in the multilateral system. The Global South bears the brunt of climate impacts, despite contributing the least to greenhouse gas emissions. Devastating floods, heatwaves and droughts have left millions vulnerable in the Global South, highlighting the urgent need for financial and technological support. Yet, the urgency seems lost on developed countries.

The outcome of COP29 has left the global climate community grappling with the stark reality of a dismal failure to deliver meaningful climate finance for the developing world. The agreement to set the New Collective Quantified Goal (NCQG) at $300 billion annually is being celebrated by developed nations as a breakthrough. However, for developing countries, this figure is a glaring reminder of the inequities entrenched in international climate negotiations. India, a steadfast advocate for the developing world, outright rejected the deal as insufficient and emblematic of the developed world's failure to honour its historical responsibilities. With catastrophic climate impacts escalating, India's resolute stance underscores the growing frustration of nations that are left to bear the brunt of a crisis they did not create, as the promises of equitable finance continue to fall woefully short.

COP29, branded as the 'Finance COP', was meant to fulfil the long-overdue commitment of establishing a new global climate finance goal to aid developing countries in their battle against climate change. This process has been nine years in the making, ever since Article 9 of the Paris Agreement in 2015 mandated developed countries to provide the necessary financial resources for mitigation and adaptation efforts in the Global South. What unfolded in Baku, however, was a glaring failure of this commitment. The paltry sum of $300 billion per year, touted as a tripling of the original $100 billion pledge, is nothing but an optical illusion, as India rightly pointed out in the closing plenary. Adjusted for inflation, the real value of the $100 billion pledged in 2009 has already eroded significantly, making this so-called 'tripling' grossly inadequate.

The real scale of funds, firmly demanded by developing countries, was $1.3 trillion annually. In fact, the report put forth by the Independent High-Level Expert Group (IHLEG) on Climate Finance puts the projected investment requirement for climate action at $2.3–$2.5 trillion per year in emerging markets and developing economies (EMDEs), excluding China. However, the final NCQG text only indicates scaling up to $1.3 trillion by 2035 'from all public and private sources' and calls on 'all actors' to do so. Furthermore, developed countries are only required to 'lead' in the mobilization of this target, effectively diluting their direct responsibility and implying that others would be required to pitch in.[1] By failing to provide non-debt-creating finance, developed countries have essentially disregarded the core principle of the United Nations Framework Convention on Climate Change (UNFCCC) which emphasizes 'equity and common but differentiated responsibilities and respective capabilities'.[2] This guiding principle acknowledges that while all nations share responsibility for addressing global environmental issues, their obligations vary based on their historical contributions to climate change and their current capacities to deal with the crisis. Developed countries, which already occupy more than 80 per cent of the global carbon budget, have failed miserably in upholding their responsibility and keeping to their commitments, and yet expect developing nations to play their part at the expense of sacrificing their SDGs.

It is time for introspection. For developing countries, the effects of climate change risk pushing an additional 100 million people below the poverty line by 2030 and are resulting in economic losses of an estimated $520 billion, according to World Bank estimates.[3] Incremental progress is no longer sufficient to tackle this escalating climate crisis. The global climate governance framework is in need of reform that prioritizes trust, equity, accountability, meaningful collaboration and implementation. Now, with the incoming Donald Trump presidency in the US, there is even more uncertainty around the outcomes of the COP.

The failure of COP29 is the latest in a long list of abdications

---

[1]Presidency text, CMA 6 agenda item 11(a): New collective quantified goal on climate finance, Version 22/11/2024, https://tinyurl.com/hss49r8u. Accessed on 4 December 2024.

[2]United Nations Framework Convention on Climate Change, United Nations, 1992, https://tinyurl.com/bdjbns6t. Accessed on 4 December 2024.

[3]US Global Leadership Coalition, *Climate Change and the Developing World: A Disproportionate Impact*, March 2021, https://tinyurl.com/2sk5ehdp. Accessed on 4 December 2024.

of the developed world in fighting climate change. The Kyoto Protocol, which was finalized in 1997 but only came into effect in 2005, was the precursor to the Paris Agreement. The US, one of the largest emitters of the world and with amongst the highest per-capita emissions, never ratified the Kyoto Protocol. Targets for emission cuts by the developed world were completely ignored, and a new narrative was taking shape—that the responsibility must be shared between the developed and developing world.[4] Now, the Global South is expected to pay for climate mitigation and adaptation, for a crisis that they have not caused.

While public debt can be an important instrument in furthering development, the Global South simply cannot afford to take on more debt to pay for the climate damage they have not contributed to. Investments in SDGs and climate action are long-term investments, requiring long-term financing. However, it is the long-term market for debt that is lacking for the Global South. Rising global interest rates in 2022 and depreciating currencies sent many countries towards debt distress. With countries in the Global South already reeling under debt, undertaking further investments in SDGs and climate actions is limited by their access to finance. According to UN Trade and Development (UNCTAD), debt servicing is now outpacing investments in critical sectors like health and education. In the 2020–22 period, 15 countries spent more on interest payments than on education, and 46 countries spent more on interest than on health.[5] Furthermore, developing nations spend more on interest payments (2.4 per cent of GDP) than on climate investments (2.1 per cent of GDP).

---

[4]Sinha, Amitabh, 'Key takeaway of COP29? The dismantling of climate talks', *The Indian Express*, 27 November 2024, https://tinyurl.com/2hanxnp3. Accessed on 4 December 2024.

[5]UN Trade & Development, *A world of debt: A growing burden to global prosperity*, 2024, https://tinyurl.com/mwt45sv7. Accessed on 4 December 2024.

Development and climate action are now becoming competing rather than complementary actions for the Global South. And the multilateral financial system, comprising institutions such as the IMF and World Bank, have failed to prevent these cascading and interlinked crises.

The failure of multilateralism to address the needs of the Global South is not only a moral failing but also a practical one. A fragmented world order cannot effectively tackle global challenges like climate change, pandemics, or economic inequality. Expanding representation of developing countries in multilateral fora is crucial. Expanding the membership of the UNSC, with a permanent seat for India and other developing countries, would expand its legitimacy. Rebalancing voting rights in multilateral financial institutions such as the IMF is another avenue to pursue. Developing economies, which will provide the bulk of global growth in the coming decades, must be given greater influence and representation. Grants and country-specific programmes must replace loans for the most vulnerable countries. Digital technologies such as DPI must be leveraged to improve governance and service delivery in developing countries, with multilateral institutions taking the lead in financing them. Transparent mechanisms for accountability of multilateral institutions and resource allocation must be put in place.

With the MDB reform agenda on the anvil, initiated by India's G20 presidency, these reforms must be implemented in a transparent and time-bound manner. A reformed, inclusive multilateral system would not only address the historical inequities faced by the Global South but also create a more stable and sustainable global order.

The key lesson here is that the Global South must work together. For too long, the voices of the Global South have been scattered and divided. The result is that our interests have been sidelined, and the developed world allowed to abdicate their responsibilities. During India's G20 presidency, India demonstrated how South–South cooperation can lead to transformative outcomes, such as the Green Development Pact, the Varanasi Action Plan to accelerate achievement of SDGs, and the inclusion of the AU as a permanent member of the G20, making it the G21. The New Delhi Leaders' Declaration enabled the concerns of the Global South to take centre stage, and this would not have been achieved if the developing countries did not work together. When the Global South allows itself to be divided, we get outcomes like that of COP 29, where not only was the scale of climate finance watered down to a third of what was required, but also the sources of funding were left ambiguous.

With global growth set to be driven by the Global South, the time has come for the Global South to unite, and push through outcomes that place their interests at the core of multilateral agreements and institutions. Only then will we be able to address critical issues such as climate change and achievement of the SDGs.

INDEX